KB196421

Korean-English Edition

STB 상생방송 「환단고기」 북 콘서트

천년 왕국
신라 역사의 재발견

Rediscovering the History of Silla

경주편

A Hwandan Gogi Lecture in Gyeongju

[한영대역]
STB상생방송 환단고기 북 콘서트 [경주편]
천년 왕국 신라 역사의 재발견

발행일	2025년 1월 13일 초판 1쇄
저 자	안경전
발행처	상생출판
발행인	안경전
주 소	대전 중구 선화서로 29번길 36(선화동)
전 화	070-8644-3156
F A X	0303-0799-1735
홈페이지	www.sangsaengbooks.co.kr
출판등록	2005년 3월 11일(제175호)
ISBN	979-11-91329-58-2
	979-11-91329-11-7 (세트)

Copyright ⓒ 2025 상생출판

Korean-English Edition

STB 상생방송『환단고기』북 콘서트 경주편

천년 왕국 신라 역사의 재발견

Rediscovering the History of Silla

안경전 · Ahn Gyeong-jeon | 지음

A Hwandan Gogi Lecture in Gyeongju

*The Origin and Hidden Truth of
a Thousand-Year Kingdom*

상생출판

§ 차 례 §

지대석

§ Contents §

【저자에 대하여 | ABOUT THE AUTHOR 】

안경전安耕田 종도사는 한민족의 고유 신앙인 증산도의 최고 지도
자다. 한민족과 인류의 시원역사와 원형문화를 밝히고 방대한 주
해와 해제까지 붙인 『환단고기』 번역·역주본(상생출판, 2012)을 출
간하였다.

AHN GYEONG-JEON, the Jongdosanim, is the supreme
leader of Jeung San Do, a native faith of the Korean people. In
2012, he published a full translated and annotated version of
Hwandan Gogi, a priceless compilation of historical records
that unveils the original history of the Korean nation—and of
all of humanity.

안경전安耕田 종도사

Ahn Gyeong-jeon
The Jongdosanim ("Supreme Leader of Jeung San Do")

신라 천 년 왕도 경주

This book is based on a lecture delivered to a Korean audience at a "Conversation with the Author" event at the Hwabaek International Convention Center in Gyeongju, South Korea, on June 12, 2016.

서론

　어젯밤 잠자리에서 신라新羅 왕국의 수도인 이 경주慶州의 역사의 근원과 숨겨진 진실을 밝히는 일은 이전의 어떤 『환단고기』 콘서트보다 훨씬 더 값진 의미가 있지 않나 생각했습니다.

　오늘 일요일 오후 즐겁게 다 같이 '이 땅의 조상들이 만들어 놓으신 위대한 역사문화의 근본정신이 무엇인가' 하는 것을 확연하게 깨쳐서 앞으로 통일 문화 역사관을 정리하는 데에 오늘 말씀의 진정한 의미가 있다고 생각합니다.

　결론은 역사 전쟁입니다. 동북아의 역사 대전쟁입니다. 근대사의 출발점에서 선언된 개벽으로 가는 역사 대전쟁입니다. 우리는 지금 이 역사 대전쟁의 중심 시간대에 살고 있습니다.

Introduction

    Last night in bed, I was thinking that revealing the origin and hidden truth of Gyeongju, the capital of Silla for a thousand years, might be a more valuable and meaningful event than any of the previous *Hwandan Gogi* book lectures. The true historical significance of today's lecture for all who have attended this Sunday afternoon with one mind lies in comprehending the fundamental spirit of the great history and culture that our ancestors built in this area and in establishing an accurate perspective of the upcoming unified culture and history.

    At issue is a war over history. It is a great war about claiming sovereignty over history in Northeast Asia. This war will lead people toward *gaebyeok* ('renewal and rebirth of heaven and earth'), which was predicted at the very beginning of modern history. We are living in the central era of the great war over the claiming of sovereignty over history.

우리는 왜 잃어버린 역사의 근원을 바르게 알고 살아야 되는가? 왜냐하면 시원 역사는 우리들의 삶의 원천이자 영감의 근원이기 때문에, 삶의 동력원이기 때문입니다. 그래서 우리의 역사의 근원과 그 창조의 힘을 바르게 깨달아야 합니다. 오늘 강연이, 우리 한민족 9천 년 역사 왜곡의 축소판인 천년 왕국 신라 역사의 근원을 바로 세우면서 진정한 한민족 역사 광복의 시간이 될 것을 소망합니다.

오늘은 왜곡되고 뿌리가 꺾여 있는 한민족 역사의 울타리를 넘어서, 동북아와 인류 창세 역사의 원형문화 정신이지만 한국 사학계의 대다수가 그토록 한 목소리가 되어 철저히 부정하고 있는 『환단고기桓檀古記』와,『삼국사기三國史記』·『삼국유사三國遺事』에 담겨 있는 한국 역사문화의 원형정신에 초점을 맞추어서 살펴보도록 하겠습니다. 이 주제를 총체적으로 깨닫는다면 이 강연이 앞으로 우리 분단 역사의 종말을 고하는 진정한 통일역사 시대의 문을 여는 계기가 될 것을 확신합니다. 우리가 이 시원 역사문화 정신을 제대로 들여다볼 수 있으면 새로운 희망의 출발점, 새 희망의 역사의 문을 최초로 활짝 열 수 있게 되는 것입니다.

아마 대한민국 국민이라면 대부분, 해외에 거주한다고 할지라도 경주를 한 번씩은 와 보잖아요? 저는 경주에 들어서면서 거대한 왕릉들을 보았습니다. 경주에는 비록 크기는 장대하지 않지만 여러 역사 유적지도 있고, 왜곡되어 있는 포석사鮑石祠라든지 첨성대瞻星臺도 있습니다. 제가 경주에 오면서, 첨성대 속에 진실로 놀라운 우주 광명 역사의 삶의 체험이 총체적으로 융합되어 있다는 것을 절감하면서, 이 신라 역사문화의 심원함과 위대함에 대해서 다시 한 번 함께 각성해야겠다는 다짐을 했습니다.

Why do we need to lead a life guided by a correct understanding of the origin of our lost history? We must do so because the history of our origin is the source of our life and inspiration, serving as the driving force of the lives we lead. Thus, we have to correctly comprehend the origin of our history and the forces behind its creation. By setting straight the distorted origin of Silla's one-thousand-year history, which itself is just a smaller version of the distortion of the Korean people's nine-thousand-year history, I hope that today's lecture will serve as an occasion for the true restoration of history for all of us.

Today, we will focus on the primordial spirit of Korean history and culture contained in *Hwandan Gogi*, *Samguk Sagi*, and *Samguk Yusa*, and hence transcend the boundaries of the distorted and broken Korean history. *Hwandan Gogi* contains the root spirit of the primordial history of Northeast Asia and humanity itself, but *Hwandan Gogi* has been radically denied by a majority of the Korean historical community. If you comprehend this subject, I am sure this lecture will be an opportunity to end our history of division and to pass through a gate into the era of a truly unified history. If we correctly understand the spirit of our primordial history and culture, this will allow us to open wide the gate of a new hope for history for the first time.

It is possible that the majority of Koreans have visited Gyeongju at least once, even those who live abroad. The huge royal tombs caught my eyes when I entered Gyeongju. In Gyeongju, there are also numerous historical sites less magnificent in scale, including Poseoksa Shrine, shrouded by a distorted narrative, and Cheomseongdae Observatory. I became keenly aware, in Gyeongju, that Cheomseongdae Observatory on the whole embodied the overall life experience of the truly amazing history of cosmic radiance, and I resolved to awaken people once again to the profoundness and greatness of Silla's history and culture.

전체적으로 볼 때 경주가 천년 왕도가 될 수 있었던 근거는 무엇이 있을까요? 크게 보면 동양문화의 기본 3요소 천문, 지리, 인사를 총체적으로 만족시키는 것이 바로 신라 역사의 토대가 아닌가 합니다. 신라가 천년 왕도를 한번 옮기려는 생각은 있었다고 하지만 실제로 옮기지는 않았습니다.

지리를 중심으로 볼 때 저 백두산에서 한반도의 척추라고 하는 태백산으로 지맥이 쭉 남쪽으로 밀고 내려오는데, 경주는 중앙에 있는 첨성대와 그 주변의 반월성半月城, 남산南山, 서쪽 선도산仙桃山, 동쪽 토함산吐含山이라든지 북녘의 산과 같은 오악五嶽이 아주 자리를 잘 잡고 있습니다.

백두대간 |
Range of Mountains Starting from
Mt. Baekdusan

Generally, why did Gyeongju become the capital of Silla for a thousand years? I am of the opinion that the history of Silla shows that it was preeminent in the basic aspects of Eastern culture: astronomy, geomancy, and human affairs. Silla is said to have once considered moving its capital, but this transfer was not enacted. From the perspective of geomancy, a long mountain range stretches south from Mt. Baekdusan to Mt. Taebaeksan, and Mt. Taebaeksan is regarded as the backbone of the Korean Peninsula. In the case of Gyeongju, Cheomseongdae Observatory is at Gyeongju's center, Banwol-seong Fortress is located not far from the observatory, and five Sacred Mountains are auspiciously positioned, including Mt. Namsan (south), Mt. Seondosan (west), Mt. Tohamsan (east), and others.

소금강산
Mt. Sogeumgangsan
177m 581 feet

선도산
390m
Mt. Seondosan
1,230 feet

첨성대
Cheomseongdae
Observatory

토함산
745m
Mt. Tohamsan
2,444 feet

단석산
390m
Mt. Danseoksan
1,230 feet

남산
468m
Mt. Namsan
1,535 feet

　지리학의 핵심 중 하나는, 물이 어디서 발원하여 어디로 빠져나가느냐 하는 것입니다. 물이 역逆 방향으로 흘러야 지리가 이루어진다고 하는데, 형산강兄山江이 경주 중심부를 흘러서 저 포항浦項으로 빠져나갑니다. 그래서 '서출동류西出東流'라는 말을 쓰는데, 지금 하동지蝦洞池를 비롯해서 물이 전부 저쪽 왼쪽에서부터 이렇게 쭉 훑어 올라와서 서쪽으로 흘러서 합수가 됩니다. 거슬러 흐르는 형국으로 해서, 한 천 년 왕도를 할 수 있는 틀이 잡혔습니다. 이 지리의 신비로움을 알고 6촌장六村長들이 여기 와서 자리를 잡았습니다.

Streams of water merge into the Hyeongsangang River, then the water reverses its course and flows into Yeongilman Bay.

One of the key focuses of geomancy are the origins and end points of water resources. The principle of the earth asserts that a river should reverse its original course to create an auspicious place. In Gyeongju, the Hyeongsangang River passes through the center of the city on the way to Pohang. Thus, the river is said to 'rise in the west and flow to the east.' All the other water resources in the region, including the Hadongji Reservoir, flow to the west and merge with the Hyeongsangang River. Thanks to the reversal of the river's flow, the way was paved for Gyeongju to become the capital of Silla that would last for a thousand years. Aware of Gyeongju's auspicious status in terms of geomancy, the heads of six villages settled there, eventually forming Silla.

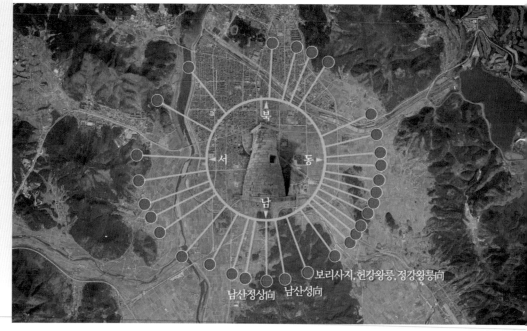

신라는 하늘의 별자리를 따라 궁궐과 왕릉을 배치했다. 출처: 울산MBC 다큐 〈첨성대 별기〉

Silla positioned palaces and royal tombs in accordance with the structure of constel-lations. (Source: Documentary "Separate Notes on Cheomseongdae Observatory")

삼원三垣 동양의 천문학에서 나누는 별자리의 세 구획. 북극 부근의 자미원(紫微垣), 사자(獅子)자리 부근의 태미원(太微垣), 뱀자리 부근의 천시원(天市垣)을 이른다.

28수 달의 움직임을 반영하여 28 구획으로 나눈 고대 동양의 별자리이다.

　　그 다음에 천문을 보면 이 우주의 삼원三垣*, 28수** 별자리를 중심으로 해서 왕도가 구성되어 있습니다. 이 우주의 전체 근본 별자리를 바로 경주, 이 왕도에 그대로 심어 놓았습니다. 그 중심에 첨성대가 있고, 주변에 여러 왕릉王陵과 주요 문화 유적지가 자리 잡고 있습니다. 이것은 수년 전에 울산 MBC TV에서 체계적으로 방영한 적이 있습니다.

　　셋째, 인사人事로는 삼국을 통일할 수 있는 문화 역사의 힘이자 토대가 화랑花郎입니다. 이 화랑 문화의 실상을 제대로 알면 신라 역사의 진정한 힘이 무엇인지 제대로 알 수 있다고 봅니다.

20

Next, in terms of astronomy, the capital was built taking into account the Three Enclosures* and the Twenty-Eight Mansions.** The arrangement of these major constellations in the universe is literally reflected in the layout of Gyeongju, the capital of Silla. In the center is Cheomseongdae Observatory, while royal tombs and major historic sites are located in the surrounding area. Some years ago, a well-organized documentary was aired on the regional branch of MBC TV in Ulsan, explaining this relationship between the constellations and the layout of historic sites in Gyeongju.

Three Enclosures. The three sections of constellations in traditional Eastern astronomy. The Three Enclosures are: the Purple Forbidden Enclosure centered on the North Celestial Pole, the Supreme Palace Enclosure near Leo, and the Heavenly Market Enclosure near Serpens.

Twenty-Eight Mansions. Ancient Eastern system of constellations. The Twenty-Eight Mansions reflect the movement of the moon rather than the sun.

Third, from the perspective of human affairs, the cultural and historical driving force and foundation that enabled Silla to defeat its rivals and unify the Three Kingdoms was the Hwarang Knights. Once we truly understand the Hwarang Knights, we will have a correct understanding of what the real power of Silla history was.

화랑! 대부분의 한국인들은 화랑을 '나라를 위해서 자신의 생명을 초개처럼 버리고 싸운 젊은 군인 조직'이라고 피상적으로 알고 있습니다. 화랑은 본래 군인이 아닙니다. 인류의 창세 문화정신을 계승한 주인공들입니다. 그들이 국가를 위해서 자원해서 목숨을 걸고 나가서 싸운 것이 화랑 문화입니다.

무엇보다도 신라 문화에서 그 역사의 근원을 찾을 때 중요한 것은 무엇인가? 이것을 서두에서, 또 마지막까지 일관되게 강조하고 싶습니다.

'신라는 진한辰韓이다.' 이것은 우리 역사의 근원을 체계적으로 바로 세울 수 있는 역사문화 주제, 근본 주제입니다.

이 진한辰韓의 실체를 알면, 천년 역사의 신라 문화와 그 창세 역사의 근원을 총체적으로, 신라 역사의 자랑스러움을 정말로 온몸으로 느낄 수 있는 그런 깨달음을 얻을 수가 있습니다.

9천 년 역사의 큰 주제는 단 한 글자로 밝을 환桓, 우주광명 환입니다. 이 우주의 광명이 크게 셋으로 나누어져서 하늘 광명과 땅 광명과 사람 광명이 되는데, 이것을 '환桓·단檀·한韓'이라 합니다. 이것을 자연수 법칙으로 천일天一·지일地一·태일太一이라 합니다. 여기에서 삼한三韓의 역사가 전개되었습니다.

환桓	단檀	한韓
하늘광명	땅광명	사람광명
천일天一	지일地一	태일太一
마한馬韓	번한番韓	진한辰韓

Most Koreans have a superficial knowledge of the Hwarang Knights as an organization of young warriors who devoted their lives to fighting for their country. However, the Hwarang Knights were originally not soldiers. They were the protagonists who inherited the spirit of humanity's primordial culture. They also voluntarily risked their lives fighting for their country.

What is the most important issue when we examine the culture of Silla for the origin of Silla's history? This must be consistently emphasized from the beginning to the end of today's lecture: 'Silla is Jinhan.' This is the fundamental focus of history and culture that will systematically set straight the origin of our history. Once we understand the reality of Jinhan, we may find an enlightenment that will allow us to comprehensively understand the origin of Silla's culture and history, which lasted for a thousand years, and feel a pride in them throughout our whole body.

The extensive content of nine thousand years of history can be summarized by just one word, *hwan*, which signifies the radiance of the universe. This radiance of the universe is generally divided into three: the radiance of heaven, earth, and humanity. These are named '*hwan*,' '*dan*,' and '*han*' respectively. Their names also incorporate the number one: "heavenly one," "earthly one," and "great one." From this concept unfolded the history of Samhan (Three Han States).

Hwan	Dan	Han
Heaven's Radiance	Earth's Radiance	Humanity's Radiance
Heavenly One	Earthly One	Great One
Mahan	Beonhan	Jinhan

그래서 역사의 근원을 잃어버리면, 특히 창세 역사의 원형문화 정신을 잃어버리면 역사의 근원과 뿌리를 상실하기 때문에 우리의 미래는 암담할 수밖에 없는 것입니다.

'역사를 잃은 자, 미래가 없다. 역사를 잃어버린 자, 패망뿐이다. 역사를 잃어버린 자, 모든 것을 잃게 된다.' 이것은 동서고금 인간 역사의 소중한 교훈입니다.

서두에서 한 가지 더 강조하고 싶은 것은, 이 신라의 왕도 경주는 '고대사와 근대사의 성지聖地'라는 것입니다. 한국 9천 년 창세 문화 역사의 세계관, 우주관의 정수를 근본으로 해서 신라가 건국되었습니다. 신라는 한반도의 동남방 모퉁이에서 끊임없는 공격을 받으면서도 이 원천적인 우주 정신문화의 근본을 바로 세우고 조직화하면서, 백성들의 문화 역사 정신으로 응집시키면서 통일을 이뤄 나갔습니다.

신한이라는 이 문화 정신을 상징히는 자랑스러운 신라 금관을 보면 그 원형문화의 상징 문양이 중심에 딱 나타나 있습니다. 어떻게 보면 뫼 산山 같기도 한데, 저것이 무엇인가? 저 속에 잠시 후에 우리가 함께 살펴보려는 아주 재미있는, 조금 충격적인 인류 창세 문화정신의 핵심이 다 들어있습니다.

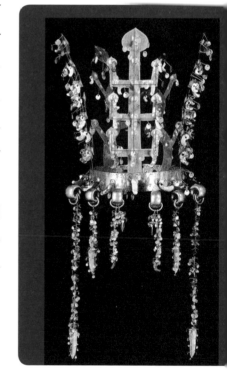

그리고 경주는 미래 부처님인 미륵불 신앙의 중심지였습니다. 석가불 중심이 아니고 미륵불을 세워서 모신, 초기 불교 사찰을 창건한 역사가 있습니다.

Losing the origin of history—losing the spirit of the primordial culture in particular—leads to the loss of the origin of history, and hence the future cannot but be bleak for those who lose these precious things.

'Those who lose their history will not have a future. People who lose their history will have nothing but failure. Those who lose their history lose everything.' This is a precious lesson from all ages and countries.

One more thing I would like to emphasize from the beginning of this lecture is that Gyeongju, the capital of Silla, was the sacred place of the ancient and modern history of Korea. Silla was established based upon the quintessence of the world view and cosmic view that runs through Korea's nine-thousand-year history and culture. Located on the southeastern side of the Korean Peninsula, Silla was under constant attack by outside forces. Despite such circumstances, Silla set right and systematically organized the foundation of the original spiritual culture of the universe and condensed it into the cultural and historical spirit of the Silla people, eventually manifesting the unification of countries on the Korean Peninsula.

We can see the pattern of Silla's primordial culture at the center of this proud gold crown of Silla symbolizing the cultural spirit of Jinhan. In some ways, it looks like the Hanja character 'san' (山, "mountain"). What is that character? In that symbol are all the key points of the spirit of humanity's primordial culture. We will examine those very interesting and somewhat striking key points in a moment. And Gyeongju was the center of faith in Maitreya, the future Buddha. In Silla's early days of Buddhism, Gyeongju historically founded a Buddhist temple where Maitreya Buddha, not Shakyamuni Buddha, was enshrined.

원형문화의 상징 신라의 금관 | 경주 황남대총 출토
A symbol of the primordial culture: A gold crown of silla excavated from the Grand Tomb of Hwangnam

유 흥 륜 사　　당 주 미 륵
有興輪寺…堂主彌勒。 (『삼국유사』「탑상塔像」)

신라 최초의 사찰, 흥륜사의 주불은 미륵불

오늘날 격동의 새로운 세계를 맞이하면서 우리 한국인의 문화 인식의 현주소를 보면 한국인은 고대사와 근대사를 보는 두 눈을 모두 상실했습니다. 9천 년 환국·배달·조선의 역사를 철저히 부정하고 뿌리 문화가 완전히 꺾여 있기 때문에 그 악업으로 근대사의 성지인 경주 땅에서 선언된 위대한 인류 현대사, 근현대사의 문화 주제인 '개벽'에 대해서도 우리가 그 뜻을 제대로 모르고 있습니다.

오늘 경주 『환단고기』 콘서트에서는 이 역사의 잃어버린 두 눈을 찾아서, 곧 닥쳐 올 남북통일의 변혁의 역사를 실제로 우리들이 제대로 깨쳐서 새 시대의 주인공이 될 것을 소망합니다. 오늘 말씀의 주제를 크게 세 가지로 잡아봤습니다.

첫째는 신라 천년 역사의 비밀, 둘째는 신라 역사·문화의 원형정신, 셋째는 통일문화를 여는 근대사의 새 울림입니다.

"The main buddha of Heungnyunsa Temple, the first Buddhist temple of Silla, was Maitreya Buddha."
(Source: "Pagodas and Buddhist Images" *Samguk Yusa*)

In today's tumultuous world, the present state of the Korean people's cultural awareness indicates that we have lost sight of both ancient history and modern history. The nine-thousand-year history of Hwanguk-Baedal-Joseon has been thoroughly denied and our cultural roots are completely severed. Due to the resulting adverse effects, we do not know the meaning of '*gaebyeok*,' the cultural focus of recent history and of the present, declared here in Gyeongju, a sacred place of modern history.

I hope today's lecture will serve as an occasion for all of you to recover a vision of history, and through that recovery to gain a correct understanding of the approaching unification of the two Koreas, so that you will emerge as main characters of the new era. I picked three subjects for today's lecture. First, "The Secrets of Silla's Thousand-Year History." Second, "The Original Spirit of Silla's History and Culture." And third, "A New Movement of Modern History to Initiate a Culture of Unification."

제1장

신라 천년 역사의 비밀

신라의 전신, 진한에 대한 왜곡

왜곡된 한국사 역사의 축소판이 신라 건국의 첫 소식에 함축되어 있습니다. 조금 전에 '신라는 진한辰韓이다'라고 했는데, 중국에서는 어떻게 왜곡을 하고 있는가?

당태종唐太宗이 고구려를 침공했다가 양만춘楊萬春 장군의 화살을 맞아 눈알이 빠지고 그 여독으로 세상을 떠났습니다. 중국 5천 년 역사에서 한나라 부제와 더불어 위대한 제왕으로 알려진 당태종이 동방 침략을 삼행했다가 그렇게 무참한 죽음을 당했습니다.

그리고서 우리 동방의 역사를 왜곡하는 여러 가지 책을 펴냈습니다.『진서晉書』,『송서宋書』,『양서梁書』같은 여러 책을 냈는데,『진서』와『후한서後漢書』에 보면, 진한은 어떤 나라인가? 중국 진시황秦始皇 때 만리장성의 노역을 피해서 이 동방으로 내려왔다고 되어 있습니다. 그래서 진한이 동방 진辰 자가 아니고 진나라 진秦 자 '진한秦韓'입니다.

당 태종 이세민李世民 | 재위 626~649

'양만춘 장군이 쏜 화살에 왼쪽 눈을 맞고(645년) 그 여독으로 사망함'

(목은 이색「정관음貞觀吟」,『태백일사』「고구려국본기」)

Chapter 1

The Secrets of Silla's Thousand-Year History

Silla's Fabricated Origin

A small portion of Korea's distorted history is the first narrative of Silla's establishment. I mentioned earlier that 'Silla is Jinhan,' and now let me explain how the Chinese distorted history. Emperor Taizong of China's Tang Dynasty lost an eyeball to Goguryeo General Yang Man-chun's arrow when Emperor Taizong invaded Goguryeo, and he eventually died of the wound. Emperor Taizong, considered one of the two greatest monarchs in China's five-thousand-year history, together with Emperor Wu (156-87 BCE) of the Han Dynasty, met with this tragic death for daring to invade the eastern land.

Later, several books were compiled that distorted the history of our eastern land, such as the *Book of Jin*, the *Book of Song*, and the *Book of Liang*. In the *Book of Jin* and the *Book of the Later Han*, what sort of state was Jinhan? These books describe the people of Jinhan as escapees from the forced labor of building the Great Wall of China for Qin Shi Huang, who came down to this land of the east. Thus, these books use the character *jin* (秦 *qin*) instead of *jin* (辰 "*east*") in referring to Jinhan.

Emperor Taizong of Tang, Li Shimin (reign 626 – 649)
He was struck in his left eye by an arrow from General Yang Manchun in 645 and eventually died of the wound. (The incident is also mentioned in the poem "Jeonggwaneum" by Yi Saek, and in "Goguryeoguk Bongi" of *Taebaek Ilsa*.)

辰韓_{진 한} 亦_역曰_왈 秦韓_{진 한} …以_이秦人_{진 인}故_고名之_{명 지}曰_왈 秦韓_{진 한}。

진한辰韓을 진한秦韓이라고도 한다. 그들이 진나라 사람인 까닭에 나라 이름을 진한秦韓이라 하였다. (『양서梁書』「동이열전」)

『진서晉書』를 보면 "자언自言호대 진지망인秦之亡人이 피역입한避役入韓하니라"라고 했고, 『후한서』에도 "진한기로자언辰韓耆老自言호대 진지망인秦之亡人이 피고역避苦役하야 적한국適韓國하니라"라고 하여 '진한의 노인들이, 우리는 노역을 피해서 도망 온 사람들이라고 했다'는 내용을 슬쩍 끼워 넣었습니다.

동북공정 현재의 중국 국경 내에서 전개되었던 모든 고대 역사를 중국 역사로 만들기 위해 2002년부터 2007년까지 5년간 중국이 추진했던, 동북 변경 지역의 역사와 현상에 관한 연구 프로젝트이다.

지금 동북공정*보다도 그 근원에서 볼 때는 더 잘못되고 악의적입니다.

自_자言_언 秦之亡人_{진 지 망 인} 避役入韓_{피 역 입 한}。

진한 사람들은 스스로 말하기를 "우리는 신秦나라에서 망명한 사람들로 진의 고역을 피하여 한韓에 들어왔다." (『진서晉書』「동이열전」)

그러니까 한반도 저 남쪽에 있는 신라도 전부 중국 사람들이 가서 지배했다는 것입니다. 신라를 중심으로 해서 볼 때 한반도는 아무것도 없고 거기도 다 중국이라는 겁니다. 그런데 『삼국사기』에 보면 그 원본이 나와 있습니다. 이 문구는 워낙 중요한데 여기 보면 "선시先是 조선유민朝鮮遺民 분거산곡지간分居山谷之間 위육촌爲六村… 시위진한육부是爲辰韓六部"(『삼국사기』「신라본기」)라 해서 '이보다 먼저 조선의 유민들이, 여기서는 단군조선이 망해서 그때 내려온 백성들이 산과 계곡에 흩어져서 살았는데 이들이 진한의 여섯 촌을 이루었다. 이것이 바로 진한 6부다'라는 것입니다. 신라의 본래 이름이 바로 진한입니다.

"Jin (辰) han is also called Jin (秦 "Qin") han.... Because they are the people of the Jin (秦 "Qin") Dynasty, the name of their country is called 'Jin (秦 "Qin") han.'" (Source: "Biography of the Dongyi" *Book of Liang*)

In the *Book of Jin,* it is written: "The Jinhan people spontaneously stated, 'We are refugees of the Jin (秦 "Qin") Dynasty and entered Han (韓) to escape from forced labor.'" And in the *Book of the Later Han*, this sentence, "The old people of Jinhan said they were fugitives who escaped from forced labor and came to the Han state" was craftily inserted. This is even more fundamentally worse and malicious than China's present-day Northeast Project.*

> "The Jinhan people spontaneously stated, 'We are refugees of the Jin (秦 "Qin") Dynasty and entered Han (韓) to escape from forced labor.'"
> (Source: "Biography of the Dongyi" *Book of Jin*)

Northeast Project. A five-year (2002-2007) research project on the history and nature of the frontier regions in Northeast China. The purpose was to claim that the history of all ancient ethnic groups or states that occupied what is now present-day Chinese territory is part of Chinese history.

This claim implies that the Chinese traveled down as far as the southern part of the Korean Peninsula where Silla was located and governed it. According to this argument, there were no political entities worthy of mention on the Korean Peninsula, except Silla, and therefore the entire area actually belonged to China. However, the truth can be found in *Samguk Sagi*. In it, this sentence is very important:

> Prior to this, refugees of Joseon [from the collapse of Dangun Joseon] scattered and lived around mountains and valleys, and formed six villages. ...(Source: "Silla Bongi" *Samguk Sagi*)

The original name of Silla was 'Jinhan.'

그런데 여기에 와서 살았던 6부, 6촌의 지배 세력은 본래 조선 유민입니다. 단군조선 역사가 망하면서 북방에서 내려왔다는 것입니다.

이 구절에서 '선시先是', 신라의 진한이 생기기 이전은 언제일까요? 『환단고기』를 보면, BCE 238년에 단군조선 마지막 47세 고열가古列加 단군이 단군 자리를 내놓고 은둔하셨기 때문에, 단군조선의 만주 영역인 진한이 그때 망해 버리고 6년 공화정으로 들어갑니다.

선 시
先是

이보다 먼저 (『삼국사기』「신라본기」)

"이 땅에 신라의 진한이 생기기 이전에" 그러니까 진한이 망한 것을 기준으로 약 180년 전부터 단군조선의 유민들이 바로 신라 땅 경주까지 들어왔으며, 신라 땅, 경주 이 지역도 본래 단군조선의 영역이라는 것입니다. 이것이 『삼국사기』에 명백히 기록되어 있습니다.

결국 해석의 문제입니다. 식민사학의 안목으로 해석할 것이냐, 본래 대한의 주체사관으로 제대로 번역할 것이냐 하는 것입니다.

Beginning 180 years before the establishment of Silla (238 BCE), Dangun Joseon refugees migrated to the land of Silla.

진한
Jinhan

신라 건국
180년 전(BCE 238)부터
단군조선의 유민들이
신라 땅까지 이주하였다

신라 Silla
경주
Gyeongju

The ruling class of the six villages who came to live here were originally refugees of Joseon. When Dangun Joseon collapsed, they came down from the northern region. Then, when was the time "prior to this"—that is, prior to the establishment of Jinhan in the Silla region? According to *Hwandan Gogi*, the last and forty-seventh ruler of Dangun Joseon, Dangun Goyeolga, stepped down in 238 BCE and secluded himself; and Jinhan, then the Manchurian region of Dangun Joseon's territory, collapsed, leading to six years of governing via a republic.

> "Prior to this [that is, prior to the establishment of Jinhan in the Silla region]..."
> (Source: "Silla Bongi" *Samguk Sagi*)

Therefore, about 180 years before the collapse of Jinhan, refugees from Dangun Joseon migrated to Gyeongju in the land of Silla, and this land also originally belonged to Dangun Joseon. This is clearly written in *Samguk Sagi*. After all, this is a matter of interpretation—a matter of whether to interpret history from a colonial perspective or a sovereign perspective.

한강 남쪽 삼한, 남삼한南三韓은 어디서 왔는가? 신채호申采浩(1880~1936)는 신라의 진한, 가야의 변한, 그리고 백제의 전신 마한 즉 남삼한은 저 북쪽에서 내려왔다고 했습니다. 북쪽 삼한에서 내려왔다는 것입니다.

그래서 이곳 신라의 첫 이름인 진한은 북쪽 단군조의 삼한에서 진한 사람들이 내려와서 형성된 것입니다. 『환단고기』에서도 이 신라의 전신을 진한으로 정의하고 있습니다.

稱國辰韓이오 亦曰斯盧라

나라 이름을 진한辰韓이라 하였고, 또한 사로斯盧라고도 하였다.

(『태백일사』「고구려국본기」)

그런데 동방 진辰 자의 실체가 아주 정확하게 중국 사서 『삼국지三國志』 「위지동이전魏志東夷傳」에 나옵니다.

지금의 역사 교과서에서는 준왕準王이 단군조의 마지막 왕으로 되어 있고 그 수도는 지금의 평양이라고 합니다. 한반도 평양이 단군조선의 수도였다는 것입니다. 그러나 실제로 단군조선의 수도 왕검성王儉城은, 만리장성이

By the way, where did the Three Han States south of the Hangang River come from? Renowned Korean historian Sin Chae-ho (1880 – 1936) asserted that the Three Han States in the southern part of the Korean Peninsula—that is, Jinhan, Byeonhan, and Mahan (a predecessor of Baekje) in the lands of Silla, Gaya, and Baekje respectively—came from the north. In other words, the Three Han States in the south migrated from the Three Han States in the north. Thus, Jinhan, located in the Silla region, was formed when people from Jinhan, one of the Three Han States constituting Dangun Joseon in the north, migrated southward. *Hwandan Gogi* also defines the predecessor of Silla as Jinhan.

> "They named the state 'Jinhan' or 'Saro.'"
> (Source: "Goguryeoguk Bongi" *Taebaek Ilsa*)

In fact, the truth of the character *jin* (辰, "east") is quite clearly shown in the "Biography of the Dongyi" chapter of *Book of Wei*, which is a constituent of the compiled text *Records of the Three Kingdoms*.

Currently, most history textbooks describe King Jun as Dangun Joseon's last ruler and its capital as present-day Pyeongyang on the Korean

남삼한南三韓
The Location of the Three Han States in the South

한강

마한
Mahan

진한
Jinhan

변한
Byeonhan

시작되는 갈석산碣石山 근교에 있는 낙랑군樂浪郡 창려현昌黎縣에 있었습니다. 당시 한나라의 연燕 지역 관리였던 위만衛滿이 번조선으로 망명하여 온지 일 년 뒤에 준왕을 내쫓고 왕검성을 차지하였습니다. 그리고 3세 후에, 위만 의 손자 우거右渠를 멸하기 위해서 한나라 무제武帝가 육군과 해군을 왕검성 으로 보냈다고 합니다. 그러고서 한반도에다가 한나라 식민지 낙랑군을 비 롯해서 한사군漢四郡, 네 개의 군을 위아래 쪽으로 세워 놓았다는 것입니다.

여기에서 역사 진실을 알 수 있는 「위지동이전」의 내용은, "초初, 우거미 파시右渠未破時, 조선상역계경이간우거불용朝鮮相曆谿卿以諫右渠不用, 동지진국東 之辰國"입니다. 우거왕 때, 정승 역계경이 간언했으나 받아들여지지 않자 망 명을 했는데, '동지진국東之辰國', 동쪽 진국으로 갔다고 했습니다. 동방에 진 국이 있었던 것입니다. 이 진국이라는 것은 원래 동방의 천자 나라, 진한(진 조선)입니다.

조 선 상 역 계 경 이 간 우 거 불 용 동 지 진 국
朝鮮相 曆谿卿 以諫右渠不用, 東之辰國。

조선상 역계경이 우거왕에게 간언했으나 받아들여지지 않자 '동쪽의 진 국'으로 갔다. (『삼국지』 「위지 동이전」)

단군조선 전체에서 북쪽 만주에 있었던 진조선이 BCE 238년에 먼저 멸 망하고, 44년 뒤인 BCE 194년에 왼쪽 날개인 번조선의 마지막 75세 기준 箕準이 위만에게 패망 당했습니다. 그래서 기준이 발해로 해서 서해를 건너 군산群山으로 들어왔습니다. 단군조선(진한)이 망한 뒤에, 위만한테 단군조 선의 왼쪽 귀퉁이 번조선을 뺏긴 것입니다.

Peninsula. However, Wanggeom-seong, the capital of Dangun Joseon, was actually located in Changli County near Mt. Jieshi (aka, 'Galseok-san'), where the Great Wall of China began. Anyway, going back to the claim of most history textbooks, at that time, Wiman, a former official of Han Dynasty's Yan region, defected to Beonjoseon, in western Dangun Joseon. A year later, he occupied Wanggeom-seong, ousting King Jun. At the time of the third ruler of Wiman's regime, Ugeo, Wiman's grandson, Emperor Wu of China's Han Dynasty sent his army and navy to Wanggeom-seong to destroy Ugeo. And then, the Four Commanderies of Han Dynasty were established on the Korean Peninsula.

Unlike the above-mentioned content of most current history textbooks, "Biography of the Dongyi" in *Book of Wei* reveals the historical truth, asserting, "At first, during King Ugeo's reign, Joseon's prime minister, Yeok Gye-gyeong, remonstrated with the king on some of his policies, but King Ugeo did not accept his ideas, so the prime minister left for the Jin State in the east." East is the direction where the Jin State was located. This Jin State was originally the nation of the Son of Heaven in the east, Jinhan (or Jinjoseon).

> "Joseon's prime minister, Yeok Gye-gyeong, remonstrated with the king on some of his policies, but King Ugeo did not accept his ideas, so the prime minister left for the Jin State in the east." ("Biography of the Dongyi" in *Book of Wei*, part of the compilation *Records of the Three Kingdoms*)

In terms of all the Dangun Joseon area: Jinjoseon located in the north—in the Manchuria region—collapsed first in 238 BCE; and forty-four years later, in 194 BCE, Beonjoseon, the left wing of Dangun Joseon, was also ruined by Wiman. Gi Jun, the seventy-fifth and last king of Beonjoseon, escaped via the Balhae Sea and crossed the West Sea to arrive in Gunsan. In summary, after Jinhan (Jinjoseon) collapsed, Dangun Joseon's left region, Beonjoseon, was taken by Wiman.

BCE 238	북쪽의 진한(진조선) 멸망
⇓ 44년 후	마한(막조선) 멸망
BCE 194	번한(번조선) 마지막 75세 기준왕, 위만에 패해 군산(익산)으로 망명

이런 역사 인식이 전혀 없이 지금 중·고등학교 교과서에 이 진국 문제를 어떻게 조작했습니까?

진국은 동쪽이 아니라, 남쪽에 있었다는 것입니다. 식민사학자 이병도가 『조선사대관』(1948)에 '남방의 진국'이라 써놨습니다. '우거는 한나라 유망인流亡人을 무제한으로 받아들이고 남방의 진국이 한漢에 교통하려 함을 방해하였다'는 것입니다. 이것을 본받아서 지금 사학계 대다수는 신라, 가야, 백제가 생기기 전에 거기에 여러 작은 성읍국가들이 있었다고 합니다. 그때 중심 세력이 생겼는데 그게 진辰이라는 것입니다. 교과서를 보면

『조선사대관』(1948)
Grand Viewpoint of Korean History

남쪽에 진이라는 세력이 있었는데 그것이 나중에 마한, 변한, 진한의 연맹체로 성장했고, 그것이 삼한三韓이라는 것입니다.

"우거왕은 ⋯ 한漢의 유민을 무제한으로 받아들이고 남방의 진국辰國이 한에 교통하려함을 방해하였다." (『조선사대관』 29쪽)

'한반도 남부 지역의 여러 정치 세력을 통합했던 나라가 진辰이었다.' (출처: <중학교 역사(상)> 36쪽, 2010년 검정. (주)지학사)

238 BCE	Collapse of Jinhan (Jinjoseon) in the north

Forty-four years later	Collapse of Mahan (Makjoseon)

194 BCE	Gi Jun, the 75th and last king of Beonhan (Beonjoseon), was defeated by Wiman and exiled to Gunsan (Iksan).

In the absence of such an awareness of history, this issue of the Jin State has been distorted in current textbooks for middle school and high schools as follows: the Jin State was located in the south, not in the east. Yi Byeong-do, a colonial historian, used the expression "the Jin State in the south" in his book *Grand Viewpoint of Korean History* (1948). His argument went: "King Ugeo... accepted drifting people from the Han Dynasty without restriction and interrupted international exchanges between the Jin State in the south and the Han Dynasty."

In accordance with his argument, a majority of mainstream historians claim that many small walled-town states existed in the area before Silla, Gaya, and Baekje were established, and from these was formed a central power, the Jin State. Their history texts assert: In the south existed a power called the 'Jin' state, which later grew to be the confederations of Mahan, Byeonhan, and Jinhan, which constituted the Three Han States.

"King Ugeo... accepted drifting people from the Han Dynasty without restriction and interrupted international exchanges between the Jin State in the south and the Han Dynasty." (Source: *Grand Viewpoint of Korean History*, p. 29)

"The state that unified several polities in the southern part of the Korean Peninsula was Jin." (Source: *Middle School History*, vol. 1, p. 36., Authorized in 2010. Publisher: Jihaksa.)

이 진국에 대해 제가 한 15년, 20년 전에 윤내현 교수의 논문을 재미있게 읽은 적이 있는데, 윤 교수는 이 진국을 어떻게 말합니까?

"갈석산碣石山에서 조선을 지나 대인의 나라를 통과하면 동쪽의 해 뜨는 곳에 이른다."는 말이 『회남자淮南子』「시칙훈時則訓」에 나옵니다. 이것은 갈석산에서 '조선' 즉 위만조선을 지나 '대인의 나라'를 통과하면 동쪽의 해 뜨는 곳에 이른다는 것입니다. '대인의 나라'가 무엇인가? 이게 진국이라는 것입니다. 진국은 중국 사서에도 동쪽에 있다고 그러잖아요.

自갈석산 過조선 貫대인지국 東지일출지동
自喝石山, 過朝鮮, 貫大人之國, 東至日出之東。

갈석산으로부터 (위만)조선을 지나 대인의 나라를 통과하면 동쪽의 해 뜨는 곳에 이른다. (『회남자』「시칙훈時則訓」)

그리고 고구려가 폐망 당한 뒤에 대중상大仲象이 후고구려를 세웠다가 뒤에 그 아들 대조영大祚榮이 국호를 대진大震이라 그랬습니다. 단군조선을 전체로 부를 때는 진국辰國이고, 그것을 나눠서 부를 때는 만주가 진한辰韓이고,

Jin State: The name of the entire region of Dangun Joseon

Concerning this Jin State, about twenty years ago, I read with interest a paper by Professor Yun Nae-hyeon, a Korean historian. In *Huainanzi*'s chapter "Shize," there is a passage: If one starts from Mt. Galseoksan, passes Joseon, and goes through the state of noble men, one reaches the east where the sun rises"; and according to Professor Yun, this eastern state where the sun rises was the Jin State. Even Chinese history texts mentioned that the Jin State was in the east.

> "If one starts from Mt. Galseoksan, passes Joseon, and goes through the state of noble men, one reaches the east where the sun rises."
> (Source: Chapter "Shize" ["Seasonal Regulations"], *Huainanzi*)

After Goguryeo collapsed and Dae Jungsang established Later Goguryeo, his son Dae Joyeong renamed the state 'Daejin.' The entirety of Dangun Joseon was called the 'Jin State.' Its constituent territories were: Manchuria, which was'Jinhan'; Dangun Joseon's left side, from west of the Luan River to the Shandong Peninsula, which was 'Beonhan'; and the entire Korean Peninsula, which was 'Mahan.' Later,

진한
Jinhan

번한
Beonhan

마한
Mahan

단군조선을
나누어 부를 때
명 칭

Names of Dangun Joseon's constituent territories

그다음에 왼쪽 요서, 산동까지가 번한番韓이고, 한반도 전체는 마한馬韓입니다. 나중에 22세 색불루索弗婁 단군 때 삼한이 삼조선三朝鮮 체제로 바뀝니다.

『환단고기』는 이것을 아주 명백하게 전하고 있습니다. 『태백일사』「삼한관경본기」에서 "총지總之하야 명왈단군관경名曰檀君管境이니 시즉진국是則辰國이오 사칭단군조선史稱檀君朝鮮이 시야是也라", 이를 총칭하여 '단군관경'이라 하니 이것이 곧 진국辰國이라 했습니다. 단군이 이 전체 영역을 다스렸고 이것이 진국이라 했습니다. 역사에서 말하는 단군조선이 바로 이것입니다.

이 『환단고기』의 역사문화 언어와, 역사문화 시대와, 역사문화의 근본정신에 대한 정의, 우주관에 근거한 정의가 얼마나 명료한지 읽으면서 감동을 받지 않을 수가 없습니다.

총 지　　명 왈 단 군 관 경　　　시 즉 진 국
總之하야 名曰檀君管境이니 是則辰國이오
시 칭 단 군 조 선　　시 야
史稱檀君朝鮮이 是也라。

이를 총칭하여 단군 관경이라 하니 이것이 곧 진국辰國이고 역사에서 말하는 단군조선이 이것이다. (『태백일사』「삼한관경본기」)

이 신라의 근원과 뿌리에 대한 역사를 볼 때 또 하나의 아주 심각한 왜곡이 있습니다. 신라의 건국시조인 박혁거세朴赫居世의 어머니가 조선 사람이 아니고 중국 사람이라는 것입니다. 이것을 『삼국유사』, 『삼국사기』에서 함께 왜곡을 하고 있습니다.

그 내용을 보면 신모神母, 이 신성하고 거룩한 어머니는 본래 중국의 제실의 따님이다. 중국 황실의 여인이라는 것입니다. 중국 사람이 와서 박혁거세를 낳았다고 했으니 박 씨들이 전부 들고 일어나야 합니다. 그런데 아직까지도 이 문제를 전혀 해결하지 못하고 있습니다.

during the reign of the twenty-second *dangun*, Dangun Saekbulru, the Three Han States were renamed the 'Three Joseon States.' *Hwandan Gogi* clearly reveals this fact. The chapter "Samhan Gwangyeong Bongi" of *Taebaek Ilsa* states, "This entire region was called 'Dangun's Territory of Jurisdiction,' and this was the Jin State. This is the very Dangun Joseon that has been mentioned throughout history."

Definitions of the language, the era, and the fundamental spirit of history and culture revealed in *Hwandan Gogi*—definitions that are based on cosmology—are so powerful and lucid that we cannot but be impressed as we read them.

> "This entire region was called 'Dangun's Territory of Juris-
> diction,' and this was the Jin State. This is the very Dangun
> Joseon that has been mentioned throughout history."
> (Source: Chapter "Samhan Gwangyeong Bongi" *Taebaek Ilsa*)

There is another serious distortion about the history of Silla's origin. It is said that the mother of Bak Hyeokgeose, the founder of Silla, was Chinese. Both *Samguk Yusa* and *Samguk Sagi* go along with this distortion. These books say that the sacred mother was originally a daughter of the Chinese imperial family. Those with the family name 'Bak' should all condemn this distortion that a Chinese woman gave birth to the founder of Silla, but this problem has yet to be solved.

신 모 본 중 국 제 실 지 녀
神母本中國帝室之女。

신모는 본래 중국 제실의 딸이다. (『삼국유사』, 『삼국사기』)

신라 역사의 근원과 뿌리에 대한 두 가지 왜곡을 다시 정리하면, 진한은 중국의 진나라 때 사람들이 와서 만들었기에 '진국秦國'이라는 것과 그 건국 시조의 어머니가 중국 여인이라는 것입니다.

『환단고기』를 보면 신라 역사에 대해서 고정관념을 깨는 놀라운 이야기가 있습니다. 그게 무엇인가? 『환단고기』 첫 편인 『삼성기』 상上을 보면 그 마무리 부분에 "부여고도夫餘故都하사… 시내신라고양야是乃新羅故壤也라", '고두막한高豆莫汗이 부여의 옛 도읍에 나라를 열었는데 그곳은 신라의 옛 땅'이라는 놀라운 이야기가 있습니다. 이 고두막한은 동명왕東明王으로 불리는데, 한나라 무제가 침공해왔을 때 그걸 꺾어버렸습니다. 지금은 고두막한이 고주몽高朱蒙으로 왜곡되어 있습니다.

고 두 막 한   진 거 부 여 고 도
高豆莫汗이 … 進據夫餘故都하사
칭 국 동 명   시 내 신 라 고 양 야
稱國東明하시니 是乃新羅故壤也라

고두막한이 … 부여의 옛 도읍을 점령하고 나라를 동명東明이라 칭하시니, 곧 신라의 옛 땅이다. (『환단고기』 「삼성기」 상)

그런데 『흠정만주원류고欽定滿洲源流考』라는 책 서문을 보면 건륭제乾隆帝가 한 말씀을 유훈으로 전하는 내용이 나오는데, "당나라 때 계림雞林으로 일컬었던 곳은 마땅히 지금의 길림吉林이란 말이 와전된 것이요, 신라·백제 등 여러 나라도 역시 모두 그 부근에 있었다."고 했습니다. 당나라 때 계림이라 했던 곳은 지금의 길림이고, 신라도 백제도 그 건국시조의 지배세력의 고향은 길림이라는 것입니다. 중국어 발음에 길림과 계림이 성조는 다르지

"The sacred mother was originally a daughter of a Chinese imperial family." (Sources: *Samguk Yusa* and *Samguk Sagi*)

As mentioned above, there are two distortions about the origin of Silla. The first one is that Jinhan is the 'Jin (秦, "Qin") State' because it was established by the people of the Jin (秦, "Qin") Dynasty of China. The second one is that the founder's mother was Chinese.

In *Hwandan Gogi*, there is an amazing story that breaks the stereotype of Silla history. The last section of *Samseong Gi I*, the first volume in *Hwandan Gogi*, describes that Godumak Han established a country in the old capital of Buyeo and that place was Silla's old land. This Godumak Han was called 'King Dongmyeong,' and he repulsed the invasion of Emperor Wu of China's Han Dynasty. Godumak Han has been distorted into Go Jumong.

"Godumak Han... advanced and conquered the old capital of Buyeo and named the state 'Dongmyeong.' This was the old land of Silla."
(Source: "Samseong Gi I" *Hwandan Gogi*)

The preface to *Manzhou Yuanliu Kao* (*"Research on Manchu Origins"*) conveys the teachings left by Emperor Qianlong, part of which asserts: "During the Tang Dynasty, the place called 'Gyerim' was a misnomer for the current Gilim. Silla, Baekje, and other countries were all also located around that area." That is, the area called 'Gyerim' during the Tang Dynasty was Gilim in *Manzhou Yuanliu Kao*'s era, and the ruling classes of Silla and Baekje were from Gilim. In Chinese, the intonations of 'Gilim' and 'Gyerim' are different, but the pronunciations are same: 'Jilin.' In this way, we can feel this truth of history via place names.

만 '지린'으로 발음이 같습니다. 우리가 역사의 진실을 지명에서도 느낄 수 있는 것입니다.

당 시 소 칭 계 림 응 즉 금 길 림 지 와
唐時, 所稱雞林, 應即今吉林之訛,
이 신 라 백 제 제 국 역 개 기 부 근 지 지
而新羅·百濟諸國, 亦皆其附近之地。

당나라 때 계림雞林으로 일컬었던 곳은 마땅히 지금(청나라)의 길림吉林이란 말이 와전된 것이며 신라·백제 등 여러 나라도 역시 모두 그 부근에 있었다. (『흠정만주원류고』 서문, 청나라 건륭제의 유지諭旨)

삼국 이전 한민족 뿌리 역사에 대한 왜곡

삼국 이전 한민족의 뿌리 역사가 왜곡되어서, 남쪽의 삼한은 북쪽의 단군조가 망하면서 그 삼한의 중심 세력들, 왕족이 내려와서 나라를 열었다는 이 진실을 대부분 모르고 있습니다. 그것은 북쪽 실체를 인정하지 않기 때문이고, 현실적으로는 단군조를 신화로 보고 총체적으로 근본을 부정하기 때문입니다.

대영박물관을 가보면 한국사 연표에 어떻게 나오고 있습니까? 구석기, 신석기, 청동기가 있고 '원삼국原三國'이라는 것이 있습니다. 'Proto-Three-Kingdoms', 원 삼국시대가 있었다는 것입니다. BCE 100년부터 CE 300년까지 400년 동안은 한반도 북부에 고구려와 남부에 신라, 백제, 가야가 성립되기 전에 원삼국이 있었다는 것인데 이게 아주 기막힌 말입니다. 그러니까 원삼국 전은 선사시대이고 단군조도 없다는 것입니다.

우리가 '중화대국주의 역사관'과 '식민사관'이라는 이 이중의 역사 왜곡의 올가미에 빠져서, 어떠한 역사학의 논리도 결론적으로 한국인은 역사의 뿌리가 신화라고 합니다. 환국·배달·조선은 다 신화이고 없는 역사라는 것입니다. 환인·환웅·단군도 신화의 인물이라 합니다.

"During the Tang Dynasty, the place called 'Gyerim' was a misnomer for the current Gilim. Silla, Baekje, and other countries were also located around that area."

(Source: Preface to *Manzhou Yuanliu Kao*, "Qing Dynasty Emperor Qianlong's Royal Message")

The Distorted History of the Korean People Before the Three Kingdoms Period

Since the root history of the Korean people before the Three Kingdoms Period has been distorted, most people are not aware of the historical truth that when Dangun Joseon in the north collapsed, its leadership and members of its royal family relocated to the southern part of the Korean Peninsula to establish the Three Han States there. Such unawareness results from the fact that most people do not recognize the existence of the Three Han States in the north and because they consider Dangun Joseon to be a myth, thus denying the root history of Korea on the whole.

By the way, what does the timeline of Korean history in the British Museum say? On that table, after the Paleolithic Age, the Neolithic Age, and Bronze Age, there is the 'Proto-Three Kingdoms' period. That is, for four hundred years, from 100 BCE to 300 CE —the time before the establishment of Goguryeo in the north, and Silla, Baekje, and Gaya in the south—there was a proto period of the Three Kingdoms. According to this ridiculous age distinction, there was a prehistoric period before the 'Proto-Three Kingdoms' and there was no Dangun Joseon period either.

Since we are trapped in the double snares of history distortion originating from Sino-centric and colonial perspectives, almost all historical logic concludes that the root of Korean history is a myth. In accordance with this logic, all the ancient countries of Hwanguk, Baedal, and Joseon were myth and not real history, and the *hwanin*s, *hwanung*s, and

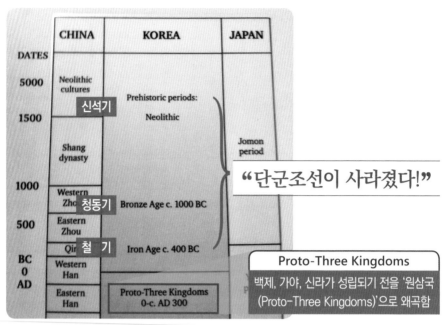

한국사 연표 | 대영박물관 한국관

　한평생, 한 생애를 바쳐 우리의 시원 창세 역사문화를 공부한 다양한 분야의 전문학자들의 총 결론이 무엇인가? 한국인은 그 근원과 조상이 없다는 것입니다. 이것이 오늘날 지구촌에 살고 있는 8,200만 한국인의 역사 인식의 현주소인 것입니다.

　하지만 학문의 어떤 정교한 논리로도, 과학주의 실증사학의 강변으로도 우리 역사의 뿌리인 환국·배달·조선의 삼성조 역사 시대를 근원적으로 부정하는 사관은 우리가 결코 용납할 수 없는 것입니다.

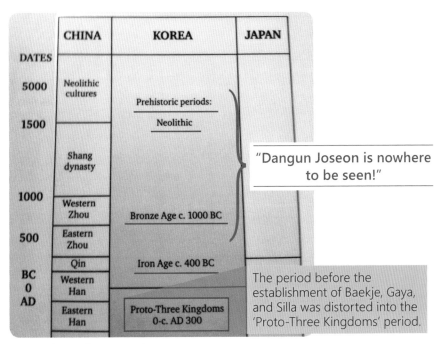

	CHINA	KOREA	JAPAN
DATES			
5000	Neolithic cultures	Prehistoric periods:	
1500		Neolithic	
	Shang dynasty		
1000	Western Zhou	Bronze Age c. 1000 BC	
500	Eastern Zhou		
BC	Qin	Iron Age c. 400 BC	
0	Western Han		
AD	Eastern Han	Proto-Three Kingdoms 0-c. AD 300	

"Dangun Joseon is nowhere to be seen!"

The period before the establishment of Baekje, Gaya, and Silla was distorted into the 'Proto-Three Kingdoms' period.

Chronology of Korean History
Korean Gallery in the British Museum

*dangun*s were also mythical characters. What is the ultimate conclusion of the research on Korean history conducted by the scholars of various specialties who devoted their lives to studying the original Korean history? Their common conclusion is that the Korean people do not have an origin and progenitors. This is the current state of historical awareness shared by 8.2 million Koreans residing across the global village.

We can never accept any view of history that basically denies our root history of Hwanguk-Baedal-Joseon or the Three Sacred Nations period no matter how elaborate the supporting logic is and no matter how sound the scientific substantiation seems.

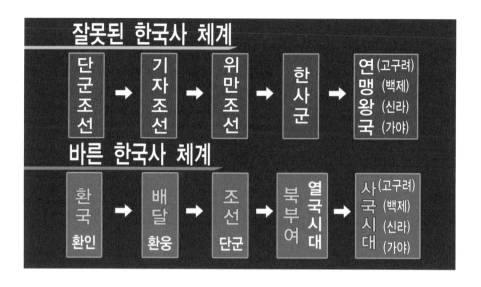

한민족의 뿌리 역사를 밝힌 『삼국유사』와 『삼국사기』

『삼국유사』와 『삼국사기』는 사실은 긍정적인 면이 더 많지만, 우리 역사를 잃어버릴 수 있는 그런 구실을 식민사학이나 농북공정을 끌고 가는 중국 사학자들에게 제공하여 한강 이남까지도 잘못하면 뺏길 수 있는, 우리 역사를 송두리째 실제로 강도질 당할 수 있는 그런 위험을 안고 있습니다. 사대주의 사서의 특성도 가지고 있는 것입니다.

이 고구려, 백제, 신라는 어떻게 탄생한 것인가? 고구려의 시조, 백제의 시조, 신라의 시조와 관련한 내용에 아주 심각한 문제가 있습니다.

신라 시조 박혁거세의 어머니가 혼전에 임신하고 옥저沃沮를 통해서, 배를 타기도 해서 이쪽 경주로 오셨다고 합니다. 그 구체적인 내용을 본론 2장에서 살펴보기로 하겠습니다. 우선 고구려 시조에 대한 문제와 신라 탄생 문제가 좀 얽혀 있기 때문에 우리가 그 뿌리를 알 수 있도록 간단하게 한번 정리를 해 보겠습니다.

『삼국사기』는 신라를 정통으로 놓기 위해서 고구려를 폄하하고, 고구려의 시조에 대한 천륜을 파괴했습니다. 그리고 고구려가 제 분수를 모르고

Erroneous Korean History System	Correct Korean History System
Dangun Joseon	Hwanguk (Ruler: Hwanin)
Gija Joseon	Baedal (Ruler: Hwanung)
Wiman Joseon	Joseon (Ruler: Dangun)
Four Commanderies of the Han Dynasty	Northern Buyeo; Many Competing States Period
Confederated Kingdoms (Goguryeo, Baekje, Silla, Gaya)	Four Kingdoms Period (Goguryeo, Baekje, Silla, Gaya)

The Root History of the Korean People Is Revealed in *Samguk Yusa* and *Samguk Sagi*

In fact, *Samguk Yusa* and *Samguk Sagi* have more positive aspects than negatives, but these books are likely to put us in danger by providing colonial historians, and the Chinese historians who are leading the Northeast Project, with excuses that can be used to claim that even the area south of the Hangang River on the Korean Peninsula was actually Chinese territory, thus taking away the entire history of the related period. In this sense, both texts have toadyism aspects.

How were Goguryeo, Baekje, and Silla established? There are serious problems with the content of these two books in regard to the founders of Goguryeo, Baekje, and Silla. The mother of Bak Hyeokgeose, the founder of Silla, became pregnant without getting married, so she left her home, traveled via Okjeo, taking a ship along the way, and finally arrived in Gyeongju. We will examine the details later. First, let me summarize the root of Goguryeo, because the progenitor of Goguryeo and the establishment of Silla were a bit entwined.

In order to claim that Silla (instead of Goguryeo) was the legitimate

감히 황제국 중국을 넘보았다고 해서 대진국(발해) 역사는 한마디도 싣지 않았습니다.

그런데 역사의 단절이 사실은 고구려의 뿌리인 동시에 백제의 뿌리, 신라의 뿌리라 할 수 있는 중간 역사의 맥이 완전히 뿌리 뽑혀 버린 데서 일어났습니다. 환국·배달·조선뿐만 아니라 단군조의 정통을 계승한 나라가 무엇입니까? 바로 **북부여**北夫餘인데, 그 **역사가 뿌리채 잘린 것**입니다. 그 결론은 무엇입니까? 고주몽의 아버지가 북부여의 건국자 해모수解慕漱라는 것입니다. 옛날 드라마에도 '고주몽의 아버지 해모수'가 화살을 맞고서 죽는 것으로 나왔습니다.

북부여의 역사는 182년인데 1세 해모수, 2세 모수리慕漱離 이후 6세까지 이어지다가, 고주몽이 계승했습니다.『환단고기』에서는 단군조를 계승한 북부여 왕조 역사의 족보를 총체적으로 밝혀 줍니다. 잃어버린 우리 한민족 9천 년 역사의 심장부, 환국·배달·조선을 북부여가 어떻게 계승해서 고구려 역사가 탄생했는가?

고주몽의 아버지는 옥저후沃沮侯 불리지弗離支인데, 불리지는 해모수의 증

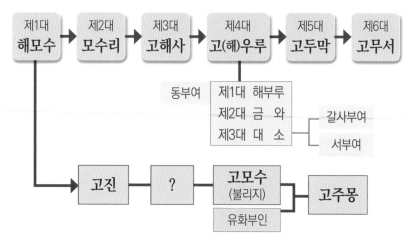

180년 북부여 왕통의 계보

successor to the dynasties of early antiquity, *Samguk Sagi* denigrated Goguryeo and distorted the family relationships of its founder. In addition, *Samguk Sagi*'s narration unfavorably asserted that Goguryeo was conceited and dared to behave insolently toward China, the emperor's state; and, reflecting this biased point of view, it did not mention a word of the history of Daejin (or Balhae) [a country founded by Goguryeo's refugees after its collapse].

By the way, the disconnection of history actually resulted from the uprooting of the middle lineage of the Korean nation's history. The term 'middle lineage' refers to the roots of Goguryeo, Baekje, and Silla. Which country inherited the legitimacy of Hwanguk, Baedal, and Dangun Joseon? That country was Northern Buyeo, but its history was completely erased. It has been said that Go Jumong's father was Haemosu, the founder of Northern Buyeo. A popular historical drama *Jumong* also described "Go Jumong's father Haemosu" as being killed by an arrow.

Northern Buyeo lasted for 182 years to be exact, from the first ruler, Haemosu, to the sixth ruler, and then Go Jumong ascended the throne. *Hwandan Gogi* reveals the complete royal genealogy of North-

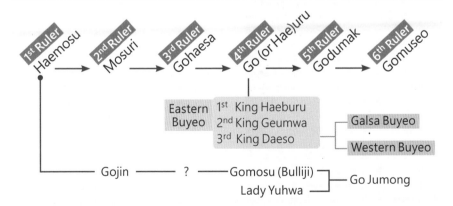

The Royal Genealogy of Northern Buyeo that Lasted for 180 Years

손자입니다. 주몽의 어머니 유화 부인柳花夫人이 혼전 임신을 하자 집안의 체면을 손상시켰다고 부모에게 쫓겨났습니다. 그래서 동부여로 떠났고 주몽은 동부여의 금와왕金蛙王 곁에서 자랐습니다.

그런데 여기서 김부식金富軾이 아주 결정적인 사대주의 역사관으로 고주몽의 두 아들, 비류沸流와 온조溫祚도 고주몽의 자식이 아니라, 우태優台라는 사람의 아들이라는 설을 실었습니다. 우태는 아내 소서노召西弩와 아들 둘을 남기고, 전쟁에 나가서 죽어버렸다는 겁니다. 주몽은 부호富豪인 연타발延陁勃의 재산을 이용하여 국가를 건설하기 위해서, 과부 소서노와 정략적으로 결혼했다는 것입니다.

그런데 『환단고기』를 보면 소서노는 연타발의 딸이 아닙니다. 바로 북부여의 마지막 왕 6세 고무서高無胥 단군의 외동딸이었습니다. 고무서 단군은 아들이 없었습니다. 고주몽이 소서노와 결혼하고 나서 나라 이름을 북부여에서 고구려로 바꿨습니다. 바꾼 이유가 무엇인가? 그 이유가 『환단고기』의 『삼성기』 끝에 나옵니다.

소서노召西弩 | BCE 66~BCE 6
북부여의 마지막 제6대 고무서 단군의 딸
(『환단고기』 「북부여기」)

Soseono (66 – 6 BCE)
A daughter of Gomuseo, the sixth and last *dangun* of Northern Buyeo.
(Source: Chapter "Buk Buyeo Gi" *Hwandan Gogi*)

ern Buyeo that succeeded Dangun Joseon. Let me tell you how Northern Buyeo succeeded Hwanguk, Baedal, and Joseon, the core and lost part of the Korean nation's history that lasted for about nine thousand years, and how Goguryeo was born.

Go Jumong's father was Bulliji, Lord of Okjeo, and Bulliji was also the great grandson of Haemosu. Jumong's mother, Lady Yuhwa, was abandoned by her parents because she became pregnant without getting married, thus bringing shame to her family. So she went to Eastern Buyeo, and her son Jumong grew up under the protection of Eastern Buyeo's King Geumwa.

However, Gim Busik, the author of *Samguk Sagi*, inserted a toadying claim that Go Jumong's two sons, Biryu and Onjo, were actually not Go Jumong's biological sons, but those of another man, Utae. According to this claim, Utae lost his life in a battle, leaving behind his wife, Soseono, and two sons. The claim further asserts that Jumong concluded a marriage of convenience with Soseono with his eye on her father Yeon Tabal's wealth so that he could use it to build a state.

According to *Hwandan Gogi*, however, Soseono was not a daughter of Yeon Tabal, but the only daughter of the sixth ruler of Northern Buyeo, Dangun Gomuseo, who did not have a son. Go Jumong married Soseono and changed the state name of Northern Buyeo to 'Goguryeo.' What was the reason? The reason is described at the end of Chapter "Samseong Gi" in *Hwandan Gogi*.

우리가 해모수 역사를 제대로 알면 신라 역사의 근원을 다 찾는 것입니다. 일본 역사의 근원을 다 찾는 겁니다. 여기에 바로 9천 년 역사의 잃어버린 국통國統을, 파괴된 역사의 근본 생명이 되는 사통史統을 바로 세울 수 있는 결정적 역사 광복의 근거가 있습니다.

『삼성기』상 마무리 부분을 보면, 고주몽이 북부여의 시조 해모수를 너무도 공경해서 '사해모수위태조祠解慕漱爲太祖'라고 했습니다. 해모수를 태조로 삼아서 제사를 올렸다는 것입니다.

사 해 모 수 위 태 조
祠解慕漱 爲太祖。

해모수를 태조로 받들어 제사를 올렸다. (『환단고기』「삼성기」상)

그런데 더 결정적인 것은 『단군세기』에 의하면 해모수가 태어난 고향이, 고향 땅 이름이 '고구려'라는 것입니다. 고구려에 대해서도 여러 가지 설이 분분하지만 하여간 본래 북부여의 시조, 해모수의 모향이 고구려이기 때문에 그 시조 할아버지, 고조할아버지를 공경해서 나라 이름을 고구려라고 했습니다.

고 구 려 내 해 모 수 지 생 향 야
高句麗 乃解慕漱之生鄕也。

고구려는 해모수께서 태어난 고향 이름이다. (『환단고기』「단군세기」)

If we gain an accurate understanding of Haemosu, this will translate into a full recovery of Silla's origin. This also touches upon finding Japan's origin. Here lies the crucial basis for restoring history, which will allow us to discover the lost link of the sovereign lineage in the nation's nine-thousand-year history, thus establishing the foundation for the nation's disconnected history. The last part of *Samseong Gi I* asserts that Go Jumong revered Haemosu, the founder of Northern Buyeo, so much that he offered ancestral rites to Haemosu, recognizing him as the founder of his country.

> "Jumong performed ancestral rites to Haemosu, revering
> him as the founder of his country."
> (Source: Chapter "Samseong Gi I" *Hwandan Gogi*)

By the way, the most conclusive evidence revealed in *Dangun Segi* is that the name of Haemosu's homeland was 'Goguryeo.' Although there are numerous theories about the origin of the state name 'Goguryeo,' Jumong named his country 'Goguryeo' out of respect for his progenitor, Haemosu, his great-great grandfather, because the homeland of Haemosu, the founder of Northern Buyeo, was Goguryeo.

> "Goguryeo was the name of the homeland where Haemosu
> was born."
> (Source: Chapter "Dangun Segi" *Hwandan Gogi*)

신라의 시조 박혁거세의 어머니는 파소婆蘇인데, 선도산仙桃山에 가면 박혁거세의 어머니인 선도산 성모를 모신 사당이 있습니다. 한무제漢武帝가 우거를 무너뜨리고서 동북아의 대천자가 되려고 했을 때 갑자기 구국의 영웅이 등장했는데 그분이 고두막한高豆莫汗입니다. 파소는 이분의 따님입니다.

일설에는 고두막한이 단군조선의 마지막 47세 단군의 후손이라고도 합니다. 이 양반이 나와서 한무제를 꺾고, 전쟁을 10년, 20년 수행했는데 당시 북부여의 4세 임금을 압박했습니다. 그 후 북부여의 4세 임금이 죽고 동생 해부루解夫婁가 등극한 후 동쪽 가섭원迦葉原에 수도를 정하고 옮겨갔습니다. 그래서 거기서 동부여東夫餘가 탄생했습니다.

그러고서 동명왕東明王이던 고두막한이 북부여의 5세 단군 자리에 오릅니다. 그러나 이 역사가 사라지고 중국에서 이 역사를 완전히 제거하자, 후세의 우리 역사가들이 그것을 미처 기록하지 못했습니다.

선도산 성모사聖母祠 | 박혁거세의 어머니 파소婆蘇를 모신 사당. 경주시
Seongmosa Shrine (Mt. Seondosan, Gyeongju)
Dedicated to Bak Hyeokgeose's mother, Paso.

Paso was the mother of Bak Hyeokgeose, the founder of Silla. On Mt. Seondosan, there is a shrine dedicated to her, the "Sacred Mother of Mt. Seondosan." When Emperor Wu of China's Han Dynasty destroyed Ugeo's regime to become the great emperor of Northeast Asia, a national hero stood up against Emperor Wu. That hero was Godumak Han, and Paso was his daughter.

According to one opinion, Godumak Han was a descendant of the forty-seventh and last *dangun* of Dangun Joseon. Godumak Han defeated Emperor Wu's invading forces, took part in numerous battles for about twenty years, and put military pressure on the fourth *dangun* of Northern Buyeo. Soon, this *dangun* died and his younger brother Haeburu was enthroned, but he was forced to relocate with his people shortly after his ascension to the throne. He built his new capital in Gaseopwon, and thus began the history of Eastern Buyeo.

After that, Godumak Han, who was the King of Dongmyeong, was crowned as the fifth *dangun* of Northern Buyeo. However, this segment of history disappeared; and later, China thoroughly deleted this segment of history, making it impossible for Korean historians of later generations to convey the related records.

북부여 제5대 단군 고두막한高豆莫汗 | 재위 BCE 108~ BCE 60. 단군조선 제 47대 고열가 단군의 후손

Godumak Han became Northern Buyeo's 5th *dangun*.
Reign 108 – 60 BCE.
Descendant of Dangun Joseon's forty-seventh ruler, Dangun Goyeolga.

이렇게 북부여의 후기 시대인 5세 고두막高豆莫 단군의 따님인 파소가 아마 혼전 임신을 해서 이 경주, 나정蘿井까지 오게 된 데에는 어떤 비밀이 있다고 봅니다. 동명왕 고두막한이 한나라 무제를 물리치고 나라를 구했지만, 동시에 북부여의 왕조를 장악해버렸습니다. 그러니까 아마 북부여 왕조의 어떤 제왕의 아들하고 파소가 연애를 해서 임신을 하니까, 그 왕실에서 '왕통을 뺏겼는데 네가 이럴 수 있느냐' 해서 거기에서 살 수가 없어서 남쪽으로 내려오지 않았나 생각해 봅니다.

박혁거세의 아버지 이름이 혹시 '사로斯盧'가 아니냐 하는 추정도 있습니다. 고주몽이 시조 할아버지 고향을 따서 나라를 고구려라 했듯이, 아마 박혁거세 어머니가 사랑한 왕자님의 이름이 사로여서 진한에서 수도를 서라벌徐羅伐로 하고 나라 이름을 사로로 바꾸지 않았겠느냐, 이런 추정도 해 보는 것입니다.

그리고 원래 백제의 시조, 사실은 최초의 여왕이라 볼 수 있는 고주몽의 둘째 부인 소서노는 북부여 마지막 6세 단군의 외동 따님입니다. 소서노가 비류沸流와 온조溫祚를 낳았습니다. 그런데 동부여에 있었던 고주몽의 첫째 부인 예씨부인禮氏夫人이 낳은 아들 유리琉璃가 아버지를 찾아오니까, 소서노는 자기 아들들에게 불리하다 해서 요동, 요서 지역으로 내려와서 어하라於瑕羅라 불리는 여왕이 되었습니다. 거기에다가 왕국을 하나 세웠지만 아들 비류와 온조가 저 인천 미추홀彌鄒忽로 왔다가, 하남河南 위례성慰禮城에서 백제의 발판을 굳히고 왕국을 열었습니다.

There must be some secret why Paso, a daughter of Northern Buyeo's fifth ruler, Dangun Godumak, who governed in the late years of his country, became pregnant without getting married and then travelled as far as this land of Gyeongju, where she allegedly gave birth to Silla's founder, Bak Hyeokgeose, beside a water well named 'Najeong.' Though King Dongmyeong, Godumak Han, repelled the invasion of Emperor Wu of China's Han Dynasty, he also seized power in Northern Buyeo. It is possible that Paso had a romantic relationship with a prince of Northern Buyeo and got pregnant, but their romance was not welcomed by the royal family of Northern Buyeo, which lost power to her father. Thus, Paso was probably forced to leave the country and travel here to the south.

There is also an assumption that the name of Bak Hyeokgeose's father may have been 'Saro.' Just as Go Jumong named his country after the homeland of his progenitor, Goguryeo, it is a possibility that the name of the prince who Bak Hyeokgeose's mother fell in love with was 'Saro,' and that the state Jinhan changed its name to 'Saro' and called its capital 'Seorabeol.'

And Go Jumong's second wife, Soseono, who originally founded Baekje and was virtually the first ruler of that country, was actually the only daughter of the sixth and last *dangun* of Northern Buyeo. As Go Jumong's queen, Soseono gave birth to princes Biryu and Onjo. When Yuri, Go Jumong's son by his first wife, Lady Ye, who had been left in Eastern Buyeo, eventually came looking for his father, Soseono had a premonition of the negative impact on her sons' future and left the country with her followers, established a country near the Yoha River (aka, the 'Liao River'), and became a ruler bearing the title 'Eohara.' Her two sons traveled down to Michuhol (present-day Incheon) and established Baekje in Wirye-seong, south of the Hangang River.

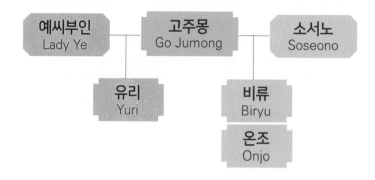

고주몽의 가계
Go Jumong's family lineage

삼국의 건국에서 얻은 결론은 무엇인가? 신라의 혈통의 근원도 북부여와 직접 연관이 있고, 고구려도 북부여의 마지막 단군을 계승한 정통 왕조라는 것입니다. 백제는 고주몽의 아들이 세웠으니까 말할 것도 없죠. 그래서 이 삼국이, 크게 보면 가야伽倻까지도 단군조의 정통을 계승한 한 형세이고, 식계로 보면 바로 북부여를 뿌리로 한 형제입니다. 신라와 고구려, 백제가 한 형제국이라는 것을 알 수가 있습니다.

『삼국유사』를 보면, 원元나라가 지구 대세를 정복하고 있을 때 거기서 충격을 받은 일연―然(1206~1289) 스님이, '도대체 우리 동방 사람은 어디서 왔는가?'라는 의문을 갖고 그 답을, 2천 년 전에 위나라 왕침王沈이 쓴 『위서魏書』를 인용해서, '지금부터 2천 년 전에 단군왕검이 아사달에 도읍을 정하고 조선을 세웠는데 요임금과 같은 때'라고 했습니다. 4천 년 전의 요임금과 같은 때라는 것입니다.

그러면 단군조선은 어디서 왔는가? 그것은 우리 기록에 없는가? 이분이 옛 기록을 봤습니다. 우리 조상들이 우리 역사문화의 옛 기록을 종합해서 써놓은 고기古記를 본 것입니다. 『해동고기』를 봤든지, 『단군기』를 봤든지, 『환단고기』의 여러 원형 고기를 봤든지 말입니다.

Nulgyeon (Jangchun),
the Capital of Goguryeo
눌견 (장춘)
고구려 수도

Paesu, Daesu regions
패수 · 대수 지역

고구려
Goguryeo

소서노(어하라)
두 아들 비류와 온조를
데리고 패대지역으로
이주 (BCE 42)

Wirye-seong in the
south of the
Hangang River
하남 위례성

Soseono (Eohara) relo-
cated to the regions near
the Paesu River and the
Daesu River with her two
sons, Biryu and Onjo (42
BCE).

온 조
소서노 타계 후
하남 위례성에 도읍
백제 건국 (BCE 19)

미추홀
Michuhol

마한
Mahan

Onjo established Baekje with its capital,
Wirye-seong, in the south of the Hangang
River after Soseono passed away (19 BCE).

What is the conclusion to be drawn from the establishment of the Three Kingdoms, Goguryeo, Silla, and Baekje? As I mentioned, the origin of the Silla Dynasty's lineage was directly related to Northern Buyeo, and Goguryeo was a legitimate dynasty that succeeded the last *dangun* of Northern Buyeo. In addition, there is no need to debate Baekje's connection with Northern Buyeo because it was established by the son of Go Jumong. Therefore, these Three Kingdoms, plus Gaya as well, were brother nations that inherited the legitimate lineage of Dangun Joseon. In terms of the direct line of descent, they were all brothers rooted in Northern Buyeo. To conclude: Silla, Goguryeo, and Baekje shared a brotherhood.

Iryeon (1206 – 1289), a Buddhist monk during the Goryeo Dynasty, was shocked when the Mongols (who also later founded the Yuan Dynasty) conquered many areas of the world, and he posed a question:

魏書에 云 乃往二千載에 有壇君王儉이
立都阿斯達하시고 開國號朝鮮하시니 與高同時니라

『위서』에 이르기를, 지금부터 2천 년 전에 단군왕검이 계셨는데 아사달에
도읍하시고 조선을 세우시니 요임금과 같은 시대였다. (『삼국유사』 「고조선」)

일연 스님이 말한 첫 마디가 무엇인가? '고기古記에 말하기를 **석유환국昔有
桓國**', 옛적에 환국이 있었다, 밝은 나라, 우주광명의 나라가 있었다는 것입

서자부 태자와 황자들을
교육했던 부서로 추정된
다.

니다. 그 가운데 서자부庶子部*의 왕자님 환웅桓雄이 동
방 태백산, 백두산에 와서 배달 신시神市를 열었다는 것
입니다.

古記에 云 昔有桓国하니

『고기』에 말하기를, 옛적에 환국이 있었다. (『삼국유사』 「고조선」)

이처럼 환국과 배달과 조선의 역사를, 국통의 큰 틀을 『삼국유사』에서
바로잡아 주고 있습니다. 물론 그 마무리에서 '일웅-熊'과 '일호-虎'라든지,
'환웅이 낳은 것이 단군이다' 해서 이 환웅의 배달 신시 역사 1,500년 역사

가 다 사라지고 그냥 '아버지와 아들의 역
사', 부자지간의 역사로 만들어 버렸습니다.

그래서 조선사편수회에서 일제 식민사학
자들이 이것을 악용하여 우리 역사의 근원,
한민족 역사의 눈알을 뽑아내고 심장을 도
려내었습니다. 환국桓國의 나라 국國 자를 쪼

일연一然 | (1206~1289)
Iryeon

'Where in the world did we, the people of the east, come from?' He then provided the answer in his book *Samguk Yusa* by quoting a sentence from the *Book of Wei*, authored by the Wei state's Wang Chen about two thousand years earlier: "Two thousand years ago, there was Dangun Wanggeom, and he made Asadal his capital and established Joseon around the same period as King Yao." This signifies that Dangun Joseon was founded about four thousand years ago.

Given this, from where did Dangun Joseon originate? Were there any Korean historical records that mentioned its origin? Iryeon checked old records about Korean ancestors, such as *Haedong Gogi*, *Dangun Gi*, and old records that served as the sources of *Hwandan Gogi*.

Department of Seoja. Presumed to have been a department that educated the crown prince and other princes.

> In the *Book of Wei*, it is written that two thousand years ago there was Dangun Wanggeom, and he made Asadal his capital and established Joseon, during the same period as King Yao. (Source: "Ancient Joseon" *Samguk Yusa*)

What was Iryeon's first statement? *"Gogi ("Ancient Records")* said that a long time ago there was Hwanguk"—that is, there was the bright country, the state of cosmic radiance. Hwanung, a prince from the Department of Seoja,* is said to have then come to Mt. Taebaeksan (present-day Mt. Baekdusan) in the eastern land and founded Baedal.

> *"Gogi ("Ancient Records")* said that a long time ago there was Hwanguk."
> (Source: "Ancient Joseon" *Samguk Yusa*)

In this way, *Samguk Yusa* set straight the overall framework of the sovereignty lineage of Hwanguk, Baedal, and Joseon. The problem with this book was that it wrongly described the Tiger Clan and the Bear

아서, 글자를 변조해서 환국·배달·조선의 40년 부족한 7천 년 역사를 부정하고, 환인·환웅·단군의 역사는 다 신화의 인물이라고 했습니다. 그런데 그 역사 말살의 족쇄를 지금 이 순간까지 우리가 전혀 풀어내지 못하고 있는 것입니다.

한국의 창세 시원사를 바로 세우는 『환단고기』

『환단고기』의 역사를 한번 간단히 정리해 보면, 『환단고기』는 다섯 분이 약 천 년에 걸쳐서 써놓은 다섯 책, 열세 권을, 조선의 3대 문호의 한 사람인 해학海鶴 이기李沂(1848~1909)와 그 제자 운초雲樵 계연수桂延壽(1864~1920)가 함께 교정을 보고 정리해서 낸 책입니다. 조선 왕조가 패망당한 그 다음 해, 얼마나 서둘러서 냈겠습니까? '이제 우리의 그 역사 뿌리를 바로 세워야 된다, 본래의 동방 우주 역사문화의 주인공의 문화정신이 나와야 된다'라고 해서 우리의 원형문화 정신을 밝히는 책을 30권 출간한 것입니다. 그런데 얼마나 곤궁했으면 홍범도洪範圖, 오동진吳東振 장군의 호주머니를 털어서 30권밖에 못 찍었겠습니까?

여천 홍범도 | 1868~1943
Hong Beom-do

송암 오동진 | 1889~1944
Oh Dong-jin

Clan as a single tiger and a single bear; and by mistakenly claiming that Hwanung fathered Dangun, it transformed Baedal's approxmiately 1,500-year-long history into merely the history of a father and son.

Then, the Korean History Compilation Committee, an organization of Japanese colonial historians, abused this book to uproot the origin of Korean history. Their act can be likened to taking out a person's eyeballs or cutting out one's heart. To name just a few issues, they denied the long history of Hwanguk, Baedal, and Joseon, which is only forty years short of seven thousand years long, by falsifying a character (*guk* ["nation"] in 'Hwanguk') in an old copy of *Samguk Yusa* and by claiming that *hwanins*, *hwanungs*, and *danguns* were all mythical figures. The problem is that Koreans have not yet broken the fetters of the Japanese colonialists' eradication of Korean ancient history.

Hwandan Gogi Sets Straight Primordial Korean History

To sum up how *Hwandan Gogi* was compiled, first, five authors wrote five volumes of books spanning thirteen chapters over a period of approximately one thousand years, then Yi Gi (1848-1909), one of the three distinguished writers of the late Joseon period, and his pupil Gye Yeon-su (1864-1920), proofread and published these chapters as a book titled *Hwandan Gogi*. The year following the Joseon Dynasty's collapse, they indeed made haste to publish thirty copies of the book, which revealed the spirit of Korean primodial culture. They published the book in the belief that the root of Korean history should be corrected and that the cultural spirit of the main protagonists of original Eastern history should be revealed. How terrible must have been their financial situation for them to print only thirty copies even though generals Hong Beom-do and Oh Dong-jin emptied their pockets!

『환단고기桓檀古記』
당대 최고의 지성 다섯 분이 천 년에 걸쳐 쓴 5책 13권의 사서

구분	삼성기 상, 하	단군세기	북부여기	태백일사
저자	안함로(신라) 원동중(고려)	고려말 이암	고려말 범장	조선 중기 이맥
소장자	계연수 (1864~1920) 백관묵(1804~?)	백관묵 이형식	이형식 (1796~?)	이기 (1848~1909)

　그런데 이것을 왜곡해서 '『환단고기』는 근세에 나왔다, 백 년밖에 안 됐다'고 합니다. 그것도 79년도 이후 80년대 초에 대중화되었기 때문에 역사서가 될 자격이 없다는 것입니다. **천 년 동안 써놓은 책을 묶어서 합본을 한 해가 1911년입니다.** 위서론자偽書論者들의 바이러스에 일절 재치기도 하지 마시고 감염되지 않기를 소망합니다.

　고려 말에 소전거사素佺居士라는 분이 비책祕冊, 고기古記를 평생 최대한 수거했는지, 그 조상되는 분들이 수거해서 자손에게 사명을 내렸는지는 모르지만, 많이 가지고 있었습니다. 소전거사는 태소암太素庵이라는 암자를 지었는데, 그 암자에서 9천 년 문화 역사 정신에 깨어 있는, 지금으로 말하면 수상까지 지낸 행촌杏村 이암李嵒(1297~1364)과, 역시 조정에 근무하며 북부여사를 전체적으로 복원시킨 범장范樟(?~1395), 그리고 이명李茗 이런 분들이 소전거사를 모시고 한민족의 역사를 복원하기로 결의동맹을 했습니다.

Hwandan Gogi

Five of the greatest intellectuals of their respective eras wrote a history text comprised of five books with thirteen chapters over a period of approximately one thousand years.

Titles	*Samseong Gi I and II*	*Dangun Segi*	*Buk Buyeo Gi*	*Taebaek Ilsa*
Authors	Anhamro (Silla Period) Won Dongjung (Goryeo Period)	Yi Am (Late Goryeo Period)	Beom Jang (Late Goryeo Period)	Yi Maek (Mid Joseon Period)
Collectors	Gye Yeon-su (1864-1920) Baek Gwan-muk (1804-?)	Baek Gwan-muk Yi Hyeong-sik	Yi Hyeong-sik (1796-?)	Yi Gi (1848-1909)

Nevertheless, many historians claim that *Hwandan Gogi* was produced in the modern era, merely one hundred years ago or so. According to them, *Hwandan Gogi* only became popular in early 1980s, which disqualifies it as a historical text. The truth is that the chapters of the five history texts were written over a period of a thousand years, and it was in the year 1911 that they were combined into one book, *Hwandan Gogi*. Hopefully, none of you will be swayed or infected with their 'contagious' claim that *Hwandan Gogi* was not a time-honored history text but a forged book of modern times.

In the late Goryeo Dynasty, a reclusive scholar, Sojeon, possessed numerous esoteric and old texts. It is not known whether he had collected those many books throughout his life or had inherited his ancestors' collections. In the Taesoam Hermitage that Sojeon built, Yi Am (1297-1364), who later served as prime minister; Beom Jang, who later also served in the government and restored the overall history of Northern Buyeo; and Yi Myeong—they all gathered together with Sojeon and affirmed their determination to restore the history of the Korean people. They had a profound awareness of Korea's nine-thousand-year history, its culture, and spirits.

소전素佺거사

고려 말, 한민족 역사·문화의 근원이 기록된 역사서를 전했다.

『단군세기』이암李嵒
『북부여기』범장范樟
『진역유기』이명李茗
　　소전素佺거사

"한민족 역사 광복을 결의동맹하다"
(1335년)

그 후 고성 이씨固城李氏 문중에서 9천 년 역사, 문화, 철학을 정리합니다.

그래서 이존비李尊庇(1233~1287), 그 다음에 이암李嵒, 이맥李陌(1455~1528), 이기李沂(1848~1909), 이유립李裕岦(1907~1986) 등 고성 이씨가 환국·배달·조선·북부여와 사국 시대, 남북국 시대, 고려의 역사 대세를 알 수 있는, 진정으로 자랑스러운 한민족과 인류 창세 문화 역사의 대의를 깨칠 수 있는 소중한 역사 경전, 문화 원전을 갖게 된 것입니다.

이 『환단고기』는 한민족의 국통 맥을 바로 세워 줍니다. 환단고기는 9천 년 역사의 국통 맥, 인류 원형문화 정신, 창세 역사를 알 수 있는 역사 경전으로서 의미가 있습니다.

Sojeon

In the late Goryeo Dynasty, he conferred history texts that recorded the origin of the Korean people's history and culture.

- *Dangun Segi*'s Author: Yi Am
- *Buk Buyeo Gi*'s Author: Beom Jang
- *Jinyeok Yugi*'s Author: Yi Myeong
- Sojeon

In the year 1335, they affirmed their determination to restore the original history of the Korean people.

Then, the Yi family, who originated from the Goseong region, put in order the history, culture, and philosophy of the Korea people's nine thousand years. To be specific, thanks to the efforts of generations that included Yi Jon-bi (1233-1287), Yi Am (1297-1364), Yi Maek (1455-1528), Yi Gi (1848-1909), and Yi Yu-rip (1907-1986), the Yi family came to possess the precious historical and cultural text that enables people to learn the flow of history from Hwanguk, Baedal, Joseon, and Northern Buyeo to the eras of the Four Kingdoms, the North-South States, and Goryeo, and to understand the proud historical origins of the Korean people and humanity's primordial culture.

This book *Hwandan Gogi* sets aright the sovereignty lineage of the Korean people. It is an important historical scripture that allows us to understand the sovereignty lineage of nine thousand years of history, the spirit of humanity's primordial culture, and the history of the world's beginning.

The sovereignty lineage of the nine thousand years of the Korean people

- **Hwanguk** (ruler: Hwanin)
- **Baedal** (ruler: Hwanung)
- **Joseon** (ruler: Dangun)
- **Northern Buyeo** (Many Competing States Period)
- **Goguryeo, Baekje, Silla, Gaya** (Four Kingdoms Period)
- **Daejin vs Silla** (North-South States Period)
- **Goryeo**
- **Joseon**
- **North-South Korea** (Division Period)

신라 왕가와 북방 유목문화

우리가 신라 왕가의 전체 역사를 보면, 박혁거세朴赫居世 시조로부터 열 분, 석탈해昔脫解를 중심으로 해서 여덟 분, 그 다음에 김씨 왕조 서른여덟 분이 나옵니다.

992년, 8년 부족한 천 년의 장구한 신라 왕조의 역사에서, 박·석·김 세 성씨를 높이는 것을, 단재 신채호는 우리의 전통문화인 본래의 삼신, 삼신문화를 의방依倣한 것이라 했습니다.

신라 왕의 성씨별 출신
56명의 왕, 총 역년 992년

시조 박혁거세는 나정蘿井 근처에서 발견된 큰 알에서 나왔다고 합니다. 석탈해는 본래 남쪽 다파라국多婆羅國에서 올라왔는데 어떤 할머니가 '하늘에서 보낸 아들'이라 해서 길렀습니다. 『삼국사기』를 보면 아주 키가 컸는가 봅니다. 그 수양어머니가 '니는 특별한 사람이다. 아주 크게 될 사람이니 학문에 정진해야 된다'고 엄정하게 얘기했습니다. 석탈해는 박혁거세의 아들하고 왕위를 놓고 겨루다가 치아가 긴 사람이 왕이 된다는 우스운 게임에서 양보를 하고서 박혁거세의 아들인 남해왕南解王의 사위가 됐습니다. 그 뒤에 왕이 됩니다. 그래서 박씨와 석씨가 융합이 되었습니다.

단재 신채호 | 1880~1936. "3성(박·석·김)을 특별히 존숭하는 것은 또한 삼신설三神說에 의방依倣한 것이다." (『조선상고사』)

Sin Chae-ho (pen name: 'Danjae,' 1880-1936) "Holding the three clan names (Bak, Seok, Gim) in great reverence was also an act of emulating the principle of Samsin." (Source: *Early History of Korea*)

The Silla Dynasty and Northern Nomadic Culture

Throughout the history of the Silla Dynasty, there were ten kings from the Bak Clan of the founder king, Bak Hyeokgeose, eight kings from the Seok Clan of Seok Talhae, and thirty-eight kings from the Gim Clan.

Renowned Korean historian Sin Chae-ho remarked that throughout the 992-year-long history of Silla, just eight years short of a thousand years, holding the three clans of Bak, Seok, Gim in reverence was an act of emulating Korean traditional Samsin culture.

Ten kings with the family name 'Bak'

Eight kings with the family name 'Seok'

Thirty-eight kings with the family name 'Gim'

Silla Kings and Their Family Names
Total: Fifty-six kings, spanning 992 years

It was said that the progenitor Bak Hyeokgeose came from a large egg found near an open well called 'Najeong.' Seok Talhae originally came from the Dapara state in the south, and an old woman adopted and raised him in the belief that he was 'a son heaven sent.' In *Samguk Sagi*, he was described as tall. His adoptive mother strictly disciplined him, saying, "You are a special person. Because you will become great, you should devote yourself to your studies." Although Seok Talhae competed with the son of Bak Hyeokgeose for the crown, Seok Talhae conceded his defeat in a rather funny contest in which the one of the two rivals with longer teeth was to be crowned, and he ended up be-coming the son-in-law of Bak Hyeokgeose's son, King Namhae. Later, Seok Talhae as-cended the throne, and thus the families of Bak and Seok were functionally merged.

제4대 석탈해昔脫解 | 재위 57~80.
박혁거세의 아들인 남해왕의 사위가 되어 등극함.
The Fourth King, Seok Talhae (reign 57-80 CE).
After becoming the son-in-law of Bak Hyeokgeose's son, King Namhae, Seok Talhae was eventually crowned.

13세 미추왕味鄒王은 첫 김씨 왕입니다. 이 김씨는 북방 유목민 가운데서 가장 강력한 흉노의 한 왕자, 한무제에게 생포됐던 그 왕자의 후손이라 합니다. 그 왕자가, 난이 일어났을 때 한무제의 목숨을 구해 주었습니다. 그 후 훈족에게는 사람 모양에 금을 입혀서 천제를 올리는 풍습이 생겼습니다.

그것을 '제천금인祭天金人'이라고 합니다. 그것은 삼신상제 천신, 아니면 『산해경山海經』에 있는 것처럼 환웅천황을 뜻하는 웅상雄像이라는 전통에서 온 것입니다. 그래서 제천금인의 풍속에 따라서 김씨 성을 줬다는 것입니다.

그 왕자가 김일제金日磾입니다. 김일제의 후손 가운데 왕망王莽이 나와서 심지어 자기 아들을 죽여 가며 대권 잡아서 나라를 빼앗아 버렸습니다. 그래서 신新나라라고 했지만 30년 만에 패망하고, 그때 김씨 왕족들이 망명해서 여기 신라와 가야에 들어왔습니다.

이 김일제의 동생이 김윤金倫인데 그 5세손 중에 형이 김알지金閼智, 바로 신라의 김씨 왕조의 시조이고, 그 동생이 김수로金首露, 가야의 시조입니다.

제13대 미추味鄒왕 | 재위 262~284.
최초의 김씨 왕, 김알지의 7세손
The Thirteenth King, Michu (reign 262 – 284 CE).
The first king from the Gim Clan.
The seventh-generation descendant of Gim Alji.

The thirteenth king, Michu, was the first Silla king from the Gim Clan. It was said that this Gim Clan were the descendants of a prince of Xiongnu, one of the strongest northern nomads. This prince, captured by Emperor Wu of China's Han Dynasty, later saved Emperor Wu's life during an attempted rebellion. Then the Xiongnu developed the custom of offering heavenly rituals that featured a golden human statue.

This custom originated from the tradition of worshipping the Heavenly God (Samsin Sangjenim) or from the tradition of *ungsang* (which symbolizes Heavenly Emperor Hwanung) as recorded in *Shan Hai Jing* ("*Classic of Mountains and Seas*"). Therefore, in light of this custom, the Xiongnu prince was said to have been granted a new family name, 'Gim' ("Gold").

The Xiongnu prince mentioned above is Gim Ilje. One of his descendants, Wang Mang, later usurped the power of China's Han Dynasty, even murdering his own son, and adopted 'Xin' as the new name of the country. The new dynasty, however, collapsed in just thirty years, and the remaining members of the Gim royal family sought refuge in Silla and Gaya. The brother of Gim Ilje was Gim Yun, and among their fifth-generation descendants were Gim Alji, the progenitor of the Silla kings from the Gim Clan and Gim Suro, the progenitor of the Gaya Kingdom.

김일제金日磾 | BCE 134~BCE 86. 흉노 휴도왕의 태자, 신라 김씨 왕족의 시조로 알려짐

Gim Ilje (134 – 86 BCE)
Xiongnu King Hudo's crown prince.
Known as the progenitor of the Silla kings from the Gim Clan.

흉노 휴도왕		
1세	김일제金日磾	김윤金倫
	⋮	⋮
5세	김알지金閼智	김수로金首露
	신라 김씨 왕조의 시조	가야 김씨 왕조의 시조

　김해에 있는 가야 수로왕과 허왕후許王后 릉을 가보면 그 뒤에 구지봉龜旨峰이 있습니다. 그런데 거기에다 고개 뒤로 넘어가는 도로를 닦느라 굴을 팠기 때문에 이후 김씨 후손 중에 큰 인물이 안 나왔다고 합니다. 그런데 김해시장이 그것을 메꾼 뒤부터 인물이 나오기 시작했다는 이야기가 있습니다. 구지봉에 올라가서 보면 그게 제사 터입니다.

　신라 역사 전체로 보면 그 역년의 반 이상을 차지하는 김씨 왕조의 왕족이, 인류 역사에서 가장 강력한 북방 유목문화를 형성하고 유럽의 역사를 평정한 흉노족 왕손이라는 것을 다시 한 번 생각해 볼 필요가 있습니다.

　신라는 1세 박혁거세朴赫居世(재위 BCE 57~CE 4) 때 '서라벌徐羅伐, 진한辰韓, 사로斯盧, 시림始林' 등 여러 국호를 쓰다가 4세 탈해왕脫解王(재위 57~80) 때 계림鷄林으로 바꾸었습니다. 15세 기림왕基臨王(재위 298~310) 때(307년)부터 국호를 신라로도 썼습니다. 여러 국호를 쓰다가 신라로 통일해 쓰기 시작한 것은 22세 지증왕智證王(재위 500~514) 때입니다. 그런데 광개토대왕 비문에 이미 신라라는 나라 이름이 나오고 있습니다.

Xiongnu King Hudo		
1st Generation	Gim Ilje	Gim Yun
	⋮	⋮
	Gim Alji	Gim Suro
5th Generation	The progenitor of the Silla kings with the family name 'Gim.'	The progenitor of the Gaya kings with the family name 'Gim.'

Behind the tombs of Gaya's King Gim Suro and his queen Heo Hwang-ok, located in modern-day Gimhae, stands Gujibong Hill. There is a folk story that asserts that the modern generations of the Gim family produced few great men ever since the hill was excavated to construct a road, thus severing the auspicious *qi* of the hill, but that after the mayor of Gimhae City had the hill reconstructed, outstanding individuals began to emerge. When I contemplate Gujibong Hill, I judge that the site in question is a proper ground for heavenly rituals. We need to be reawakened to the fact that the kings with the family name 'Gim,' whose combined reign years are longer than half of Silla's entire dynastic era, are the descendants of the Xiongnu who established the strongest northern nomatic culture in history and dominated European history.

Silla used various country names—such as 'Seorabeol,' 'Jinhan,' 'Saro,' and 'Sirim'—during the reign of its first ruler, Bak Hyeokgeose (r. 57 BCE – 4 CE), and it changed the country name to 'Gyerim' at the time of the fourth ruler, King Talhae (r. 57 – 80 CE). The name 'Silla' began to be used in the year 307 CE, during the reign of its fifteenth ruler, Girim (r. 298 - 310). 'Silla' was eventually selected as the sole official country name at the time of its twenty-second ruler, King Jijeung (r. 500 – 514). However, on the stele of Goguryeo's King Gwanggaeto, the name 'Silla' had already appeared.

신라의 국호 변천

1세 박혁거세	서라벌 徐那伐, 진한辰韓 사로, 시림
4세 탈해 이사금	시림에서 계림으로 변경
15세 기림왕	307년 신라新羅 국호 사용 시작
22세 지증왕	503년 신라로 국호 통일

신라의 원뜻은 '덕업일신德業—新 망라사방網羅四方'입니다. 여기에는 '덕업이 새로운 나라, 밝은 햇살, 천지의 광명이 온 천하를 덮으소서' 하는 기도의 뜻이 담겨 있다고 합니다.

'신라' 국호의 의미

덕 업 일 신 망 라 사 방
德業日新 網羅四方。

덕업이 날로 새로워지고 천지광명이 온 천하를 덮으소서

(『삼국사기』「신라본기」)

탈해왕은, 신라 김씨의 시조가 되는 김알지를 '하늘에서 나에게 보낸 아들이다' 하며 길렀는데, 하여간 김씨와 석씨가 자연스럽게 한 가족이 되는 내용이 정말로 신비스럽습니다.

신라 30대 문무왕文武王(재위 661~681) 비문에도, 우리 조상 할아버지는 '투후제천지윤秺侯祭天之胤'이라는 말이 있습니다. 황하가 굽이친 오르도스 지역의 투후로서, 아주 강력한 제후로 봉함을 받은 김일제, 즉 흉노 왕손의 후손이라는 것입니다. 문무왕이 직접 '우리 조상은 북방 유목민 흉노의 왕손'이라고 밝힌 것입니다. 이 김씨가 참 무서워요. 당해 내기 어려운 북방의 아주 강력한 유목문화의 기동력과 전사의 피가 김씨들의 생명 속에 흐르고

Silla's Country Name Changes	
1st Ruler, Bak Hyeokgeose	Seorabeol, Jinhan, Saro, Sirim
4th Ruler, Talhae	The name 'Sirim' changed into 'Gyerim.'
15th Ruler, Girim	Started using the name 'Silla' in the year 307 CE.
22nd Ruler, Jijeung	Various country names were unified as 'Silla' in the year 503 CE.

The name 'Silla' suggests a prayer: "May more and more new virtuous works be accomplished day by day so that the radiance of heaven and earth will cover the entire world."

The Meaning of the Country Name 'Silla'

May more and more new virtuous works be accomplished day by day so that the radiance of heaven and earth will cover the entire world.
(Source: "Silla Bongi" *Samguk Sagi*)

Gim Alji, the progenitor of Silla's Gim Clan, was raised by King Talhae, who considered Gim Alji to be 'a son heaven sent to me.' This story of the Gims and Seoks naturally coming together to become one family is indeed mysterious. The epitaph of Silla's thirtieth ruler, King Munmu (r. 661-681), explains that his ancestors were "descendants of the Lord of the Ordos region, who performed heavenly rituals." This means that his ancestors were descendants of Gim Ilje—a powerful enfeoffed lord of the Ordos area encircled by a rectangular bend of the Yellow River, and also a member of the Xiongnu royal family. The epitaph is equivalent to King Munmu's personal statement that his ancestors were royal offspring of northern nomadic Xiongnu. The Gims are indeed tough. In their genes, they have the northern nomadic culture's unparalleled mobility and warrior spirit.

투후 秺侯	오르도스 지역의 제후
제천 祭天	하늘에 제사를 올리던
지윤 之胤	흉노 왕족(김일제)의 후손

있는 것입니다.

가락국 본문에서 언급된 가야를 지칭하며, 금관 가야라고도 한다.

가락국駕洛國* 왕의 역사를 보면 허왕후許王后가 시집 와서 자기 남편에게 시집오게 된 실제 이야기를 합니다. 『삼국유사』를 보면, '우리 아버지 어머니가 사실은 천상의 상제님에게 명을 받았다. 저 동방에 있는 가락국 시조를 하늘에서 내가 내려 보냈으니 네 딸을 그쪽으로 보내서 왕비가 되게 하라'고 했다는 이야기가 있습니다.

그런데 가야와 형제가 되는 신라의 김씨 왕족의 역사에서 어떻게 당나라 와 친해져서 형제국 백제를 멸망시키고 고구려를 멸망시켰는가? 그것이 진 정한 통일인가? 이 문제는 우리가 역사를 배우면서 좀 불편하게 느낍니다.

신라의 삼국통일에 대해서는 이 지역에 사는 사람이나 후예들도 좀 떳떳 하지 못한 자책감이라고 할까, 콤플렉스를 느끼고 있습니다. 그런데 북방 유목문화의 근본정신을 한번 들여다보면, 당시 중국 당나라 왕조의 혈통 을 같이 생각해 보면 이해할 수 있는 역사 해석의 여지가 생긴다고 봅니다.

秺侯 Tuhu	Feudal lord the Ordos region.
祭天 Jecheon	Performed heavenly rituals.
之胤 Jiyun	Were descendants of a Xiongnu royal family member (that is, Gim Ilje).

According to the dynastic history of the Garak State,* King Gim Suro's queen, Heo Hwang-ok, told her husband, after they married, the story of what led her to marry him. Regarding this, *Samguk Yusa* conveys a narrative of what she allegedly said. She said that her parents actually received a mandate from Sangjenim in heaven. And Sangjenim said that he had sent the progenitor of the Garak State in the east from heaven, and that they should send their daughter to him to become his queen.

Garak State. Another name for the Gaya Kingdom mentioned in the text. Also known as 'Geumgwan Gaya.'

How did it happen that Silla's royal family of the Gims, whose progenitor was the brother of the progenitor of Gaya's royal family, destroyed brother countries like Baekje and Goguryeo in collusion with China's Tang Dynasty? Can this be called a genuine unification? When we think of this question as we learn about the associated history, we, as Koreans, feel uncomfortable.

Concerning the issue of such a unification of the Three Kingdoms by Silla, even the descendants of Silla's royal family, the Gim Clan, and other people who live in this region seem to have some sort of guilty conscience or guilt complex about it. However, when the basics of northern nomadic culture and the blood lineage of China's Tang Dynasty at that time are also taken into account, we can reasonably understand this history.

북방 유목문화의 특성

이 유목문화는 지구촌의 동서남북의 문화를 소통하는 진정한 개척자로서, 문화 소통자로서 역할을 했습니다. 유목민은 야만인이 아닙니다. 말 타고 가축을 몰고 이동한다고 해서 문화가 없었던 것이 아닙니다.

유목문화의 꽃은 무엇인가? 유목문화의 정화精華는 황금문화인데, 실제로 우리가 지구촌 여기저기를 가보면, 스키타이라든지 저 몽골 서북쪽에 있는 소련 땅 파지릭이라든지 아프가니스탄, 여기저기의 황금문화를 보면 깜짝 놀라지 않을 수가 없습니다.

유목문화를 한평생 연구한 서울대 김호동 교수가 최근에 유목문화를 종합 정리한 『아틀라스 중앙 유라시아사』라는 아주 멋진 역사책을 냈습니다. 그에 따르면 지구촌의 유목 강국들은 공통적으로 3수 의식이 있습니다. 그래서 나라를 셋으로 나누어 다스립니다. 몽골도 그렇고, 흉노도 그렇고, 선비도 그렇습니다. 전체적으로 보면 3수의 정신에 따른 좌현왕左賢王·우현왕右賢王이 있고, 그 밑에 군 조직에 우방과 좌방이 있고 24장의 조직을 가지고 있습니다.

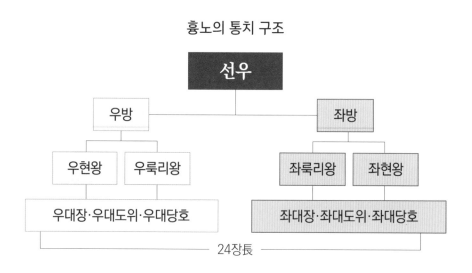

흉노의 통치 구조

The Characteristics of Northern Nomadic Culture

This nomadic culture played the role of cultural communicator and true pioneer conveying cultures in all directions across the global village. Nomads are not barbarians. Even if they moved on horseback with livestock, that did not mean they had no culture. What was the flower of nomadic culture? The culmination of nomadic culture was gold relics. Indeed, if you travel from place to place in the global village, you cannot help being startled by the golden relics of the Scythians, the Pazyryk from the northwest of Mongolia, and Afghanistan.

Professor Kim Ho-dong of Seoul National University, who has researched nomadic culture for a lifetime, recently published a great book of historic interest entitled *Atlas of Central Eurasian History*, a comprehensive text on nomadic culture. According to him, many powerful nomads in the history of the global village shared the custom of setting much value on the number three. Thus, they divided their states into three parts and ruled accordingly. For example, the Mongols, the Xiongnu, and the Xianbei all had such traditions. In general, they had a ruling system in line with the custom of valuing the number three, comprised of the Wise King of the Right and Wise King of the Left under the Chanyu. Their military also had Right and Left Wings and organizations of twenty-four leaders.

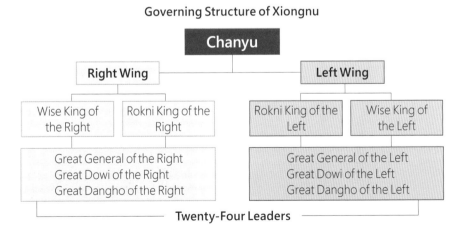

Governing Structure of Xiongnu

동방 유목문화권 스키타이족의 황금빗 I
BCE 4. 러시아 에르미타주박물관.
A Scythian golden comb from the eastern
nomadic culture (4 BCE)
The State Hermitage Museum, Russia

15마리 금제 그리핀(봉황) 장식 I
얼음공주, 알타이 파지릭 2호분
Ice Princess with fifteen golden griffin
(phoenix) decorations
Altai Pazyryk ancient tomb #2

특별전 [황금의 아프가니스탄] | 2016년 4월~6월, 동경국립박물관
Special Exhibition (Golden Relics from Afghanistan)
April 12 –June 19, 2016, Tokyo National Museum

북방 유목문화는 그 유물을 보면 신라, 가야 유물과 상통하는 것이 있습니다. 편두偏頭를 하고, 기마상을 보면 동복銅鍑을 말 등에 싣거나, 말 엉덩이 위에 지고 다닙니다.

동복도 제대로 잘 보면 삼신의 3수 문양으로 되어 있습니다. 제가 러시아 답사를 할 때 한 유목 문화권 박물관을 가니까 지구에서 가장 큰 동복이 있었습니다. 몇 천 명 밥을 해 먹을 수 있는 그런 거대한 동복도 봤습니다.

또한, 지금까지 전 세계에서 금관이 한 열 개 나왔다고 하는데, 그중에 여덟 개가 바로 신라에서 나왔습니다. 여러 무덤에서 나온 신라의 금관은 인류의 원형문화, 우주 역사의 원형정신을 담고 있습니다.

신라의 금관 문화에 나오는, 우주 창세 역사문화의 어떤 최상의 상징, 우주의 진정한 수수께끼를 저는 곡옥曲玉이라고 봅니다. 곡옥은 참 아름답고, 어떻게 보면 귀엽기도 하고 신비스럽습니다. 뭔가 신성한 기운이 있습니다. 이것을 태아의 모습, 물고기 모습이라 해석하기도 합니다.

지금 서울에 있는 대한 독립문을 보면 그 위에도 태극 형상으로 그린 문양이 있습니다.

황남대총 금관
Gold crown from the Grand Tomb of Hwangnam

Remains from northern nomadic culture and from the cultures of Silla and Gaya show they had many things in common. They shared the custom of flattening the head, and their relics of equestrian statues showed that they carried a bronze cauldron on the back or rump of their horses.

Careful examination of this cauldron also reveals patterns of the number three associated with Samsin. When I visited a museum dedicated to nomadic culture during my field survey in Russia, I saw probably the largest bronze cauldron in the world—one that could feed thousands.

It is known that about a dozen or so gold crowns have been excavated worldwide; and among these, eight crowns are from Silla. Gold crowns from Silla tombs disclose the primordial culture of humanity and the original spirit of cosmic history.

I am of the opinion that the comma-shaped beads are a supreme symbol of the history of the world's creation or a true cosmic enigma related to the gold relics of Silla. Comma-shaped beads are very beautiful, adorable in some aspects, yet mysterious. There is sacred energy in them. Some explain their shape as that of a fetus or a fish.

In the upper part of the pattern of the Independence Gate in Seoul is emblazoned a symbol depicting Taegeuk in the form of comma–shaped beads.

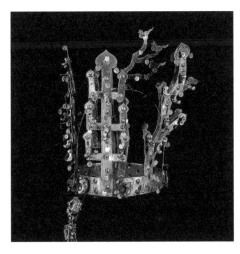

서봉총 금관
Gold crown from Auspicious Phoenix Tomb

북방 유목문화의 영향을 보여주는 유물, 편두偏頭
Flattened heads are relics showing the influence of northern nomadic culture.

가야의 편두 유골 |
Skulls of flattened heads in Gaya

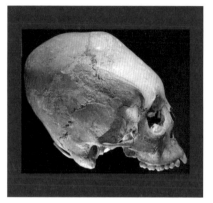

흉노의 편두 유골 |
Skulls of flattened heads in Xiongnu

북방 유목문화의 영향을 보여주는 유물, 동복銅鍑
Bronze cauldrons are relics exhibiting the influence of northern nomadic culture.

신라 기마상의 동복 |
A bronze cauldron on a Silla equestrian statue

흉노의 동복 |
A bronze cauldron of Xiongnu

삼신의 삼수문양을 한 동복

Bronze cauldrons with patterns of "three pieces as one set" associated with Samsin

러시아 국립역사박물관 |
The State Historical
Museum of Russia

(흑해)로스토프박물관 |
Rostov Museum
(near the Black Sea)

(흑해)크라스노달박물관 |
Krasnodar Museum
(near the Black Sea)

대형 동복 BCE 6
우크라이나 헤르손주 출토
키예프 역사박물관

Large bronze cauldron (6 BCE), excavated in the Province of Kherson.
National Museum of the History of Ukraine in Kyiv

이 곡옥이 무엇인가? 곡옥이라는 말은 일본 사람들이 만든 술어입니다. '구부러진 옥'이라는 뜻인데 사실은 유치한 말입니다. 일본 사람들이 '마가 타마まがたま'라고 하는데 이게 아무런 의미가 없습니다. 어떻게 보면 이것 도 식민사학의 연장선에서 나온 용어입니다.

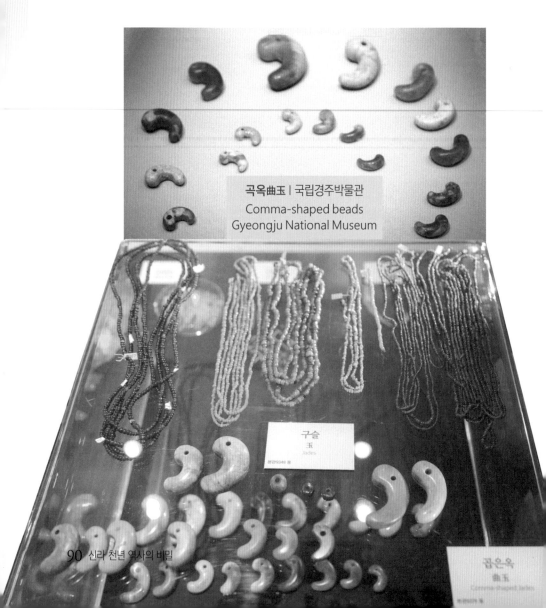

곡옥曲玉 | 국립경주박물관
Comma-shaped beads
Gyeongju National Museum

구슬
玉
Jades

곱은옥
曲玉
Comma-shaped Jades

These comma-shaped beads are also called 'curved jade,' which is a term coined by the Japanese that carries little meaning. In some respects, this term arose from the effects of colonial history.

곡옥 형상의 태극 |
Taegeuk in the shape of comma-shaped beads

독립문 |
Independence Gate

중국에서는 5,500년 전에서 한 9천 년 전의 광의의 홍산문화, 진정한 동북아의 인류 창세 역사문화의 유적지가 나왔습니다. 거기에서 나온 문화의 상징이 용봉龍鳳입니다. 초기에는 옥으로 만든 용을 곡옥이라 하지 말고 옥룡玉龍이라 부르자고 했습니다. 우리나라의 강우방 교수 같은 분은 절대 곡옥이라는 말을 쓰지 말자고 합니다. 곡옥이라는 말은, 그냥 생긴 형상이 구부러진 옥이라는 뜻이니까 아무런 의미가 없는, 어린이 코흘리개들 수준의 용어라는 것입니다.

　　사실 북방 유목문화의 유물을 보면, 아주 재미있는 문화 정신이 나타나 있습니다. 예를 들어서 신라의 김씨 왕에게 보낸 황금 보검이 있는데 그 황금 보검을 보면 무엇이 있습니까? 거기에 **삼태극**三太極이 있는데, 이 삼태극 문양을 바로 구부러진 곡옥처럼 새겨 놓았습니다.

우하량牛河梁**유적** | 중국 요령성 건평현
5,500~9,000년 전 인류 창세문화인
홍산문화의 중심 유적지

제단
Altar

무덤
Tomb

Niuheliang Archeological Site
The central remains of the Hongshan culture,
the primordial culture of humanity's origin,
from 5,500 to 9,000 years ago.
(Jianping County, Liaoning Province, China)

In China, an archaeological site was found that is from the Hong-shan culture in a broad sense, and which dates back 5,500 to 9,000 years, a site of the true primordial culture of humanity in Northeast Asia. Cultural symbols found at the site include the dragon and the phoenix. Earlier, some people insisted the term 'curved jade' not be used, insisting on 'jade dragon.' Korean professor Gang Wu-bang, an art historian, asserts that we should not use the term 'curved jade,' which merely describes the shape of the jade artifacts and is therefore a meaningless and childish term.

In fact, a very interesting cultural spirit is revealed in the artifacts of northern nomadic culture. For example, on the ornamental gold dagger sent to a Silla king of the Gim Clan is a tripartite Taegeuk, and the tripartite Taegeuk is engraved in a fashion similar to comma-shaped jade.

황금보검의 삼태극 |
The tripartite Taegeuk on the ornamental gold dagger

신라 황금보검 | 경주 계림로 출토, 국립경주박물관, 5~6세기
Ornamental gold dagger from Silla (fifth to sixth century) Excavated from Gyerim Road, Gyeongju (Gyeongju National Museum).

저런 문양의 원상原象은 무엇일까요? **우주광명 환桓**에서 분화된 하늘·땅·인간에 살아있는 삼신의 신성, 그것을 천일天─·지일地─·태일太─이라고 합니다. 바로 이 우주의 조물주의 생명과 신성이 3수로 표현되는 것입니다.

그래서 **천일·지일·태일, 하늘 광명·땅 광명·인간 광명**을 저렇게 구분해서 삼태극 양식으로 새긴 것이라 해석하는 것이 바람직하지 않은가 생각해 봅니다.

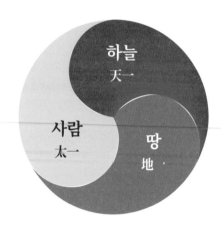

황금보검의 삼태극

조물주의 생명과 신성		
천일天─	지일地─	태일太─
하늘광명	땅광명	사람광명

3수로 분화되는 것을 삼태극 양식으로 표현

What would be the original image of the tripartite Taegeuk pattern? Samsin's divinity is alive in the three entities of heaven, earth, and humanity, which branched from the cosmic radiance *hwan*, and these are named 'Heavenly One,' 'Earthly One,' and 'Great One' respectively. That is, the vitality and divinity of the universe's creator is expressed through the number three. Thus, it would be reasonable to interpret the inscribed tripartite Taegeuk pattern as an expression of Heavenly One, Earthly One, and Great One, or of heavenly radiance, earthly radiance, and human radiance.

The tripartite Taegeuk pattern on the ornamental gold dagger

The Vitality and Divinity of the Creator.		
Heavenly One	Earthly One	Great One
Heavenly Radiance	Earthly Radiance	Human Radiance

The differentiation into three entities was expressed as the tripartite Taegeuk pattern.

그 다음으로 신라에서 나오는 적석목곽분積石木槨墳이라는 무덤이 있습니다. 러시아의 파지릭에서 발굴된 유사한 형태의 무덤에서는 얼음공주의 유물과 미라가 나왔는데, '알타이 고분 얼음공주'라고 해서 노보시비르스크에 있는 박물관 한쪽에 전시되어 있습니다.

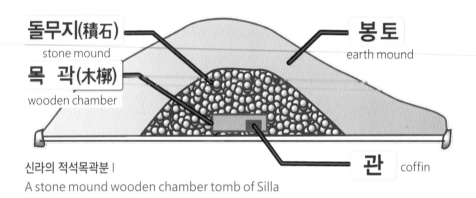

신라의 적석목곽분 |
A stone mound wooden chamber tomb of Silla

얼음공주묘 | 알타이 파지릭 2호분 → 신라와 동일한 적석목곽분
Altai Pazyryk tomb #2 (the tomb of Ice Princess)
→ the same design as Silla's stone mound wooden chamber tombs

Next, there are stone mound wooden chamber tombs excavated in Silla. A similar type of tomb was excavated in the Pazyryk Valley, Russia, where a mummy dubbed the 'Siberian Ice Princess' and artifacts were found. The mummy was introduced as the "Ice Princess from an ancient tomb of Altai" and displayed in a corner of a museum located in Novosibirsk, Russia.

얼음공주 전시 모형 | 러시아 과학원 시베리아 분원 박물관
The exhibition of an Ice Princess replica
Siberian Branch of the Russian Academy of Sciences

여기서 나온 '쿠르간'의 목관을 그대로 옮겨다 놓은 게 있습니다. 피터 대제가 처음 개척한 한때의 수도인 저 러시아의 서부, 페테르스부르크 박물관 지하관을 가보면, 그 거대한 관을 그대로 옮겨 놓았습니다. 해가 져서 문 닫기 전에 서둘러 그곳을 방문했는데, 아주 큰 목관木棺을 그대로 옮겨 놓고 거기에 왕이 타던 말의 모습을 새겨 놓았습니다. 그 말의 목에 곡옥이 있었습니다. 그게 그렇게 신비스럽습니다. 그리고 그 목관에서 나온 동방 문화의 표지標識 유물이 여러 가지 있었습니다.

북방 유목민 왕의
대형 목곽
에르미타주 박물관

Nothern nomad king's huge wooden chamber
The State Hermitage Museum

They excavated and moved in its entirety a huge coffin of a king from a nomadic culture, transferring it from a kurgan to a basement exhibition hall in a museum in St Petersburg, western Russia, once the capital of Russia after Peter the Great (1672 – 1725) claimed the land for the first time. I rushed to the museum before its closing time and saw the huge wooden coffin with the carving of a king's horse with comma-shaped jade hanging from the horse's neck. It looked so mysterious. And many artifacts representative of eastern culture were found in that coffin.

우주광명문화를 상징하는 유물 |
곡옥曲玉
Comma-shaped jade
An artifact symbolzing the
culture of cosmic radiance

에르미타주박물관 | 상트 페테르부르크
The State Hermitage Museum, St Petersburg

그런데 이 유목문화는 어디에서 유래했는가? 흉노 즉 훈족이 됐든, 선비족이 됐든 그들은 우리와 조상이 같지 않습니까? 지금 튀르키예도 그 조상은 투르크, 돌궐족입니다. 돌궐족 후손들이 내려가서 오스만제국을 열고 동로마 제국을 멸망시켜 버렸습니다. 칭기즈칸의 군대는 러시아, 인도에 이르기까지 이 세계의 절반을 지배했습니다.

그러면 몽골, 선비라든지, 돌궐, 흉노 이들은 어디에서 유래했는가? 이 기록을 찾을 수 있는 것은 『단군세기』밖에 없습니다.

『단군세기』에 따르면, 3세 가륵嘉勒 단군이 열양列陽 욕살褥薩인 삭정索靖의 잘못을 벌하여 감숙성으로 귀양을 보냈습니다. 그 후에 삭정을 사면하여 왕으로 임명하였고, 삭정은 흉노의 시조가 되었습니다.

4세 오사구烏斯丘 단군은 자신의 동생을 몽골의 초대 왕으로 임명했습니다. 3세 단군 때는 강거康居가 반란을 일으켜서 단군께서 지백특支伯特을 평성했는데, 강거는 돌궐의 시조입니다. 이런 역사가 『단군세기』에 나오고 있습니다.

By the way, where did this nomadic culture originate? Whether no-mads were the Xiongnu—that is, the Huns—or the Xianbei, did they not share ancestors with Koreans? The ancestors of current Turkey were the Turks, or Gokturks. The descendants of the Gokturks relo-cated to establish the Ottoman Empire and to destroy the Byzantine Empire. Genghis Khan conquered half of the world, including Russia and India. So where did the Mongols, Xianbei, Gokturks and Xiongnu originate? *Dangun Segi* is the only history text that records this part of history.

The third ruler of Dangun Joseon, Dangun Gareuk, exiled Sakjeong, the governor of the Yeolyang region, to Gansu Province due to his misdeeds. Later, Dangun Gareuk pardoned Sakjeong and appointed him as a king there, which allowed him to become the progenitor of the Xiongnu.

The fourth ruler, Dangun Osagu, appointed his younger brother the first king of the Mongols. The third *dangun* had suppressed a rebellion of Ganggeo in Jibaekteuk. Ganggeo was the progenitor of the Gok-turks. This part of history is mentioned in *Dangun Segi*.

진한
Jinhan

Yaksu River
(Ruo River)

감숙성 약수弱水
Gansu Province

Beonhan
번한

Mahan
마한

『단군세기』제3세 가륵단군

욕살 삭정索靖을 약수에 유배 후 그 땅에 봉함.
삭정이 흉노의 시조가 됨 (BCE 2177)

Governor Sakjeong was exiled to the Yaksu River region and was later enfeoffed there. Sakjeong became the progenitor of the Xiongnu (2177 BCE).
(Source: Section on the third *dangun*, Gareuk, in *Dangun Segi*)

대세를 보면 이 동서 유목문화의 큰 세력권은 바로 환국·배달·조선을 계
승한 동방 우주광명 문화, 삼신사상, 우주사상을 가지고 있습니다. 그 심
장부인 단군조에서 행한 삼신 우주광명 통치제도를 '삼한관경三韓管境'이라
하는데, 삼한으로 나라를 나누어서 국가 영역을 다스린 것입니다. 이 유목
문화를 보면, 좌현왕·우현왕 제도 같은 삼한관경 문화를 대부분 가지고 있
습니다.

어사달
봉지封地
enfeoffed region to Osadal

진한
Jinhan

Yaksu River
약수弱水

Beonhan
번한

Mahan
마한

「단군세기」 제4세 오사구단군
동생 오사달烏斯達을 몽고리한蒙古里汗으로 임명
(BCE 2137)

Osagu, the fourth *dangun*, appointed his younger brother, Osadal, as King of the Mongols (2137 BCE).
(Source: Section on the fourth *dangun*, Osagu, in *Dangun Segi*)

In general, the big powers of the nomadic cultures of the East and West inherited the Eastern culture of cosmic radiance, the concept of Samsin, and the cosmology of Hwanguk, Baedal, and Joseon. The system of governing based on the cosmic radiance and Samsin culture practiced in Dangun Joseon was called the 'Territory of Jurisdiction Partitioned into Three Han States.' This term means they governed the state's territory by dividing it into Samhan ("Three Han States"). People of the nomad cultures usually had a tradition of governing the territory by partitioning it into three, such as the systems of the Wise King of the Left and the Wise King of the Right.

주요 신라왕

신라는 신교를 모체로 해서, 전통문화를 모체로 해서 유교도, 불교도 받아들이고, 도교와 함께 융합해서 신라 천년 역사를 만들어나갔습니다.

1세 박혁거세. 중심 세력인 6촌장이 박혁거세朴赫居世(재위 BCE 57~CE 4)를 왕으로 모시고 나라를 다스렸고, 2세 남해왕南解王(재위 4~24)은 석탈해昔脫解를 사위로 삼고, 중국 호칭인 왕 대신 '거서간, 차차웅, 이사금'이라는 호칭을 썼는데 이 호칭은 전부 **우두머리, 혹은 광명을 상징**합니다.

그 다음에 13세 미추왕味鄒王(재위 262~284)은 김알지의 7세 후손이며, 김씨 성을 가진 최초의 신라 왕입니다.

17세 내물왕奈勿王(재위 356~402) 때부터 김씨 왕위가 세습되어서 왕통은 성골*에서만 나오고, 진골**은 왕이 될 수가 없었습니다.

성골 부모가 모두 왕족 출신인 신분.
진골 부모 중 한쪽이 왕족 출신인 신분.

김춘추金春秋(603~661)와 김유신金庾信(595~673)은 진골이기 때문에 왕이 될 수 없었지만, 신라의 정치를 근본적으로 혁신해서 삼국통일의 꿈을 이루기 위해서 아마 두 사람이 서로의 누이와 딸을 배우자로 삼는 혈맹을 통해서 삼국통일의 초석을 다졌다고 봅니다.

김유신金庾信 | 595~673
가야 김수로왕의 12세손.

Gim Yusin (595 – 673)
- A twelfth-generation descendant of Gaya's King Gim Suro

Major Silla Kings

With Spirit Teaching and traditional culture as its basis, Silla accepted Confucianism and Buddhism and fused with Daoism to create its history, which spanned almost one thousand years. The first ruler was Bak Hyeokgeose. The heads of six villages, who were the central authority of the people, crowned Bak Hyeokgeose (r. 57 BCE – 4 CE) as king to rule their country.

The second ruler, Namhae (r. 4 – 24), made Seok Talhae his son-in-law and used the monarchical titles 'Geoseogan,' 'Chachaung,' and 'Isageum' instead of the Chinese-style title 'Wang ("King").' The titles he used generally symbolized "leader"or "radiance."

Later, the thirteenth ruler, Michu (r. 262 – 284), was Gim Alji's seventh-generation descendant and the first Silla monarch with the clan name 'Gim.'

At the time of the seventeenth ruler, Naemul (r. 356-402), the Gim Clan began to bequeath the throne to their descendants, and only those of the *seonggol* * social class could succeed to the throne, while those of the *jingol*** social class were not qualified to ascend the throne.

seonggol. "Hallowed bone." People whose parents both descended from the royal family.
jingol. "True bone." People with one parent who had descended from the royal family.

Since Gim Chunchu (603 – 661) and Gim Yusin (595 – 673) were from the *jingol* class, they were not qualified for the crown; but, aspiring to unify the Three Kingdoms by bringing innovative changes to Silla's politics, they laid the groundwork for the unification of the Three Kingdoms via a blood alliance through which they offered a daughter and a sister to each other respectively as spouse.

주요 신라왕
Major Silla Kings

제1세 박혁거세朴赫居世 | 재위 BCE 57~CE 4
칭호: 거서간居西干

The first ruler, Bak Hyeokgeose
(r. 57 BCE – 4 CE)
- Monarchical title: 'Geoseogan'

제2세 남해南解왕 | 재위 4~24
칭호: 차차웅次次雄

The second ruler, Namhae
(r. 4 – 24 CE)
- Monarchical title: 'Chachaung'

제13세 미추味鄒왕 | 재위 262~284
최초의 김씨 왕, 김알지의 7세손

The thirteenth ruler, Michu
(r. 262 – 284)
- The first monarch with the clan
  name 'Gim'
- The seventh-generation descendant of Gim Alji

제17세 내물奈勿왕 | 재위 356~402
김씨 왕위 세습(성골)
칭호: 마립간麻立干

The seventeenth ruler, Naemul
(r. 356 – 402)
- The Gim Clan started to inherit the throne.
  Only those of *seonggol* ("hallowed bone")
  class could succeed the throne.
- Monarchical title: 'Maripgan'

제23세 법흥法興왕 | 재위 514~540
The twenty-third ruler,
King Beopheung (r. 514 – 540)

제27세 선덕善德여왕 | 재위 632~647
The twenty-seventh ruler,
Queen Seondeok (r. 632 – 647)

제29세 무열武烈왕 | 재위 654~661
The twenty-ninth ruler,
King Muyeol (r. 654 – 661)

제30세 문무文武왕 | 재위 661~681
The thirtieth ruler,
King Munmu (r. 661 – 681)

제56세 경순敬順왕 | 재위 927~935
The fifty-sixth ruler,
King Gyeongsun (r. 927 – 935)

그 다음에 23세 법흥왕法興王(재위 514~540) 때 이차돈異次頓 순교 사건이 나오는데, 신라는 불교를 쉽게 받아들이지 않았습니다. 3세기 초에 고구려 사람 아도阿道 승려가 내려오기도 했지만, 신교 우주광명 전통사상 세력과 새로운 불교 혁신 세력 사이에 끊임없는 충돌과 갈등이 있었습니다. 그러다가 마침내 이차돈이 희생자로서 순교를 하고, 그 이후로 불법을 국가 경영 정신의 근본으로, 호국불교護國佛教로 만들어나갔습니다. 그렇다고 해서 석가모니를 중심으로 섬긴 것만은 아니었습니다. 우리가 신라라고 하면 불교를 떠올리고, 석가모니를 주불로 생각하지만 실제로 반드시 그런 것은 아니었습니다.

그리고 27세 선덕여왕善德女王(재위 632~647) 때부터 통일의 기반을 실제로 닦았다는 지적이 있습니다.

통일을 처음 이루기 시작한 김춘추 즉 29세 무열왕武烈王(재위 654~661) 때 나당羅唐 연합군이 백제를 멸망시켰습니다.

김유신의 부계는 가야의 왕족이었는데 신라에 귀부歸附해서 공을 세웠습니다.

김유신은 열다섯 살 때 화랑이 되었고 그 후에 기도하면서 신인으로 하늘의 인증을 받았다고 합니다. 김유신이 천상 33천의 천신의 한 사람으로 지상에 내려왔다는 이야기가 역사서에도 나옵니다.

그리고 김춘추의 아들 30세 문무왕文武王(재위 661~681) 때 통일이 이루어지고. 마지막 56세 경순왕敬順王(재위 927~935) 때 신라 왕조가 마무리됩니다.

During the reign of the twenty-third ruler, King Beopheung (r. 514 – 540), the martyrdom of Ichadon took place. When Buddhism was first introduced, Silla would not easily accept it. In the early third century, Ado, a Buddhist monk of Goguryeo, came to spread Buddhism, but there were constant conflicts between the practitioners of traditional thought regarding cosmic radiance and Spirit Teaching and the new revolutionary Buddhists. After Ichadon was ultimately martyred, Silla made Buddhism the basic principle of state management and further developed Buddhism as a defender of the state. Nevertheless, they did not worship just Shakyamuni as the main buddha. When we think of Silla, we immediately think of Buddhism and of Shakyamuni as the main buddha, but actually it was not always so.

By the way, it has been said that the groundwork for the unification of the Three Kingdoms was actually laid during the time of the twenty-seventh ruler, Queen Seondeok (r. 632 – 647).

During the reign of Gim Chunchu—or the twenty-ninth ruler, King Muyeol (r. 654 – 661)—Silla began unifying the Three Kingdoms by first destroying Baekje via an alliance with China's Tang Dynasty.

Gim Yusin's paternal line was the royal family of Gaya. They performed meritorious deeds after surrendering to Silla.

Gim Yusin became a leader of the Hwarang Knights at age fifteen and is said to have been later certified by heaven as a divine person through his prayers. According to one history book's account, Gim Yusin was one of the heavenly spirits of the Thirty-three Heavens, who descended to earth.

The unification of the Three Kingdoms was achieved during the reign of Gim Chunchu's son, King Munmu, the thirtieth ruler (r. 661 – 681).

The Silla Dynasty came to an end at the time of the fifty-sixth ruler, King Gyeongsun (r. 927 – 935).

신라의 불교문화

신라의 불교문화를 보면, 우선 아도阿道 화상이 미추왕 2년, 263년에 고구려에서 자기 어머니 고도녕高道寧의 명을 받아서 신라에 왔습니다. 아도의 어머니는 유명한 승려와 연애를 해서 아들을 뒀는데, 그 아들을 다섯 살 때 출가를 시켰습니다. 아마 도승이 되기를 원했던 모양인데, 그 뒤에 '앞으로 3천 개월 후에 동국에 불법을 크게 흥왕하게 하는 성군이 나온다. 그러니까 너는 거기에 가서 불교의 개조開祖가 돼라'고 했습니다.

시기	불교 정착 과정
미추왕 2년(263)	고구려 승려 아도가 고도녕의 명에 의해 서라벌로 들어옴 → 신라에 불교 전래
법흥왕 14년(527)	이차돈의 순교 → 불교를 국교로 공인
신흥왕(540~576)	신라 불교의 중흥기
진평왕(589)	수나라와 외교관계를 맺고 불교를 적극적으로 수용

그래서 아도가 신라에 들어왔는데 3년 뒤에 공주의 병을 고쳐주고 왕의 신임을 얻습니다. 그러고서 자기 소원은, 절을 지어 불교를 크게 일으키는 것이라 했고 그래서 흥륜사興輪寺를 지었다고 합니다.

제가 답사를 해 보니까 흥륜사는 지금의 경주공업고등학교 자리에 있었고 그것이 신라 최초의 절터입니다.

아도阿道 화상 |
고구려 승려로 신라에 불교를 들여옴(263년)
Venerable Monk Ado
A Buddhist monk from Goguryeo, he introduced Buddhism to Silla in the year 263.

The Buddhist Culture of Silla

Regarding the introduction of Buddhism to Silla, a Buddhist monk, Ado, came from Goguryeo to Silla in the second year of King Michu's reign (263) following his mother's advice. His mother, Go Donyeong, had fallen in love with a well-known Buddhist monk and given birth to a son. She sent her son to a monastery at the age five, probably wishing him to become a great monk. Years later, Go Donyeong prophesied to her son, "In three thousand months, a wise king will appear in the eastern nation to lead Buddhism to great prosperity, so you should go there to become the progenitor of Buddhism."

Period	The Settlement Process of Buddhism
The 2nd year of King Michu's reign (263)	Goguryeo Buddhist monk Ado entered Seorabeol following Go Donyeong's advice. ⇨ Buddhism was introduced to Silla.
The 14th year of King Beopheung's reign (527)	Martyrdom of Ichadon ⇨ Buddhism was certified as a state religion.
King Jinheung (r. 540 – 576)	The golden age of Silla Buddhism
King Jinpyeong (589)	After the establishment of diplomatic relations with the Sui Dynasty in China, Silla actively accepted Buddhism.

Hence, Ado went to Silla, and three years after entering Silla, Ado healed a princess's illness, gaining royal trust. He said his wish was to build a Buddhist temple and bring great prosperity to Buddhism. Thus, Heungnyunsa Temple was built.

Heungnyunsa Temple, which used to be located at the site of the current Gyeongju Industrial-Technical High School, was the first temple site of Silla. Right in front of the school's main building, a lotus pedestal and several pillars still remain from the old temple site.

그 학교의 본관 건물 바로 앞을 보면 예전의 절터에 연화대도 있고 여러 가지 기둥이 아직 많이 남아 있습니다.

	원형 불교시대 절터	신라가 세운 사찰
1	천경림天鏡林	흥륜사
2	삼천기三川岐	영흥사
3	용궁남龍宮南	황룡사
4	용궁북龍宮北	분황사
5	사천미沙川尾	영묘사
6	신유림神遊林	천왕사
7	서청전婿請田	담엄사

안내판 | Information Board
"It is speculated that the site of Gyeongju Industrial-Technical High School was the location of Heungnyunsa Temple (established in 544), the first Buddhist Temple of Silla...."

Temple Sites Before the Days of Shakyamuni Buddha		Temples Built by Silla
1	Cheongyeongnim	Heungnyunsa Temple
2	Samcheongi	Yeongheungsa Temple
3	Yonggungnam	Hwangnyongsa Temple
4	Yonggungbuk	Bunhwangsa Temple
5	Sacheonmi	Yeongmyosa Temple
6	Sinyurim	Cheonwangsa Temple
7	Seocheongjeon	Dameomsa Temple

흥륜사 터 연화대 |
경주 공업고등학교

A lotus pedestal at the Heungnyunsa Temple site Gyeongju Industrial-Technical High School

신라에는 석가 부처님이 오시기 전 원래 원형原型 불교가 있었다고 하는데 그런 절터가 일곱 개나 있습니다.

그 터는 역사적으로 바로 **신교의 제천 소도蘇塗** 터인데 여기에 전부 절을 세워나간 것입니다. 이것은 무엇을 말하는가? 이것이 바로 우주광명 전통 신교문화의 성지, 천신 기도터에 불교가 자리 잡아 나가는 과정이라는 지적은 아주 합리적인 역사 해석이라고 봅니다.

신라의 불교 정착 과정을 보면 아도 화상이 미추왕 2년에 들어오고, 약 3백 년 뒤에 이차돈의 순교 사건이 있었습니다.

이웃 나라 일본에는 불교 정착 과정에 갈등이 컸습니다. 그 갈등은 소가(蘇我) 집안과 모노노베(物部) 집안 사이에 일어났습니다. 모노노베 집안에서는 '우리들이 모시는 국신國神은 본래 조선에서 왔고, 이 천신을 모시는 신사문화로 만족해야 된다'고 했습니다. 그런데 소가 집안은 '불교를 받아들여야 된다'고 했습니다. 그래서 막 싸웠는데 모노노베 집안에서 소가 집안에 쳐들어가서 집안에 만들어 놓았던 절을 파괴하고 불상을 끌어내어 바다에 던져 버렸습니다. 그리고 나중에는 소가 집안이 모노노베 집안을 멸족시켜 버립니다.

고대 일본의 양대 씨족

물부物部씨(모노노베)	대립	소아蘇我씨(소가)
국신國神(삼신상제)파		숭불崇佛파

신라에서는 이런 처절한 갈등이 아니라 비교적 순리적으로 불교의 정착이 이루어졌습니다. 미추왕 때 아도가 들어왔지만 아도는 뜻을 이루지 못하고 홀로 죽어버렸습니다.

그리고 나서 한 5백 년 세월 동안은, 천지의 광명을 가지고 나라를 다스

It has been said that Silla had a primordial form of belief predating Shakyamuni Buddha's advent and that there were seven of those temple sites. Those sites were historically *sodo*s where Spirit Teaching's rituals for heaven used to be held, and on all of those sites were later built Buddhist Temples. What does this mean? It seems a very reasonable historical interpretation to say that a process occurred in which Buddhism became entrenched on the sacred sites of cosmic radiance culture, of traditional Spirit Teaching, or on the sites of prayer to Heavenly God. In summary, the founding process of Buddhism in Silla involved a Buddhist monk, Ado, entering Silla in the second year of King Michu's reign, and about three hundred years later, Ichadon's martyrdom took place.

In the case of the neighboring country, Japan, large conflicts broke out between the Soga Clan and the Mononobe Clan over the arrival of Buddhism. The Mononobe Clan insisted that the state's God was originally from Joseon and therefore it was enough to simply worship this Heavenly God, while the Soga Clan asserted that the Japanese should accept Buddhism. Thus, the two clans eventually clashed: the Mononobe Clan attacked the Soga Clan, destroying the Buddhist temple in their compound and casting their Buddha statues into the sea. Later, the Soga Clan exterminated the Mononobe Clan.

Two Major Clans of Ancient Japan

Mononobe	← Conflict →	Soga
A sect revering the God of the state (Samsin Sangjenim)		A sect revering Buddhism

In the case of Silla, the founding of Buddhism went ahead relatively reasonably, without such severe conflicts. During the reign of King Michu, Ado came to Silla, but he failed to accomplish his goal and died alone. For some five hundred years afterward, certain cultural

린 단군조선 진한의 역사 주체정신, 즉, 우주광명 문화의 진정한 주인정신 같은 진한의 문화역사 전통이 이어졌습니다. 그러면서 화랑 문화의 한계를 극복하려는 과정에서 당나라에 대한 사대주의 역사로 흐르게 된 것입니다. 일반적으로 이렇게 해석할 수 있다고 봅니다.

신라의 수도 경주는 미륵 신앙의 성지

그런데 신라 불교는 단순히 석가불을 중심으로 한 불교가 아닙니다. 화랑 문화를 보면, 화랑은 각자가 '화랑은 미륵의 화신이다'라는 미륵의 심법으로 미륵의 이상낙원을 건설하는 주인공이었습니다.

신라 역사의 초기에는 백제, 고구려, 그리고 왜적들이 자주 습격을 하여 약탈을 하고 백성을 학살했습니다. 그래서 『삼국사기』를 읽다 보면 신라가 당했던 고통을 엿볼 수가 있습니다. 처음에 남삼한이 자리 잡을 때는 북쪽에서 번조선의 탁卓 장군이 내려와서 마한을 세우고, 남쪽 삼한의 진왕辰王이 됐어요. 백제의 전신인 마한의 왕이 그 세력이 강성했기 때문에, 진왕으로서 변한과 진한의 종주 역할을 했습니다. 삼한은 항상 일체였는데 신라가 진한의 역사정신과

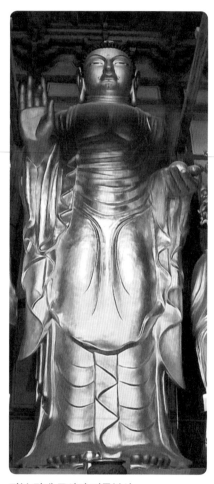

전북 김제 금산사 미륵불상
Maitreya Buddha statue
Geumsansa Temple, Gimje, Jeollabuk-do Province

traditions continued, for example Jinhan's nature as the main protagonists of history, and the spirit as the genuine master of the cosmic
radiance culture. And Jinhan of Dangun Joseon was the focus of governing the nation by means of heaven and earth's radiance, and it was
also the center of history.

In the process of searching for ways to transcend the limitations of
the Hwarang Knights, however, Silla fell into a posture of toadyism
toward the Tang Dynasty of China. I am of the opinion that this is a
generally accepted interpretation of that part of history.

Gyeongju, the Capital of Silla: A Sacred Site of Maitreya Faith

By the way, Silla's Buddhism did not center on worshipping Shakyamuni Buddha. According to Silla's Hwarang Knights, each of the
Hwarang Knights was regarded as an incarnation of Maitreya, and
they were the main protagonists who were armed with Maitreya's
mindset and were to build Maitreya's paradise on earth.

In the early days of Silla, there were a lot of pillaging and massa-
cres due to surprise attacks by Baekje, Goguryeo, and Japan. We can
glimpse the hardships that Silla endured in passages from *Samguk
Sagi*. At the time when the Three Han States relocated to the southern
part of the Korean Peninsula, General Tak of Beonjoseon came down
from north to establish the Mahan state and played the role of a de
facto king of all the Three Han States in the south, which were dubbed
'Jin.' Because the King of Mahan, which was the precursor of the
Baekje kingdom, was politically powerful, he served as the suzerain
of both the Byeonhan and Jinhan states as the King of Jin. The Three
Han States had maintained a bond between themselves and acted like
one entity, but as Silla began to recognize the historical awareness
and cultural spirit of Jinhan, Silla realized that the center of the Three
Han States' history was not the King of Jin or the King of Mahan, but
themselves. Concerning Jin, modern mainstream historians devalue

문화정신을 회복하면서, 원래 우리 역사의 중심은 마한 진왕이 아니고 '우리들 자신'이라는 의식을 갖게 되었습니다. 그것을 지금 강단사학자들은 남쪽에 진辰이라는 나라, 혹은 진이라는 어떤 세력이 있었다고 추정될 뿐이라고 교과서에서 평가절하 하였습니다.

신라의 왕도 경주는 미륵신앙의 성지입니다. 이 신라의 미륵신앙은 어찌 보면 자랑스럽고, 어찌 보면 새롭다고 할 수 있습니다. 신라 천년 불교문화의 근본을 바로 세우는, 또 삼국을 통일하는 역사의 추동력이 어디서 나왔는가? 물론 화랑의 실체도 중요하지만 '미래에 이 세계를 근본적으로 혁신하고 개벽을 하는 도솔천 천주님 미륵불이 이 땅에 오신다, 미륵불이 이 땅에 오신다'는 믿음에서 온 것입니다.

전륜성왕 정법正法을 가지고 온 세계를 다스릴 것이라는 인도 신화의 이상적 왕.

전륜성왕轉輪聖王*을 꿈꾼 진흥왕眞興王은 자기 두 아들을 '동륜銅輪', '사륜舍輪'이라 했습니다. 신라뿐만 아니라 백제도 26세 성왕聖王이, '내가 바로 미륵님의 이상을 성취하는, 용화낙원을 세우는 전륜성왕'이라는 의식을 갖고 있었습니다. 그래서 일본에서는 백제의 성왕을 성명왕聖明王이라고 합니다.

이 미륵신앙이 돈독했기 때문에 신라의 초기 왕대에 도솔가兜率歌라는 전통음악이 나왔습니다. 그 노래 제목이 왜 도솔가인가? 도솔천 미륵에 대한 신앙은 어디서 발원이 된 것인가? 정말로 신비스럽지 않을 수가 없습니다.

신라에서는 미륵선화彌勒仙花인 미시랑未尸郞의 전설이 등장하는데, 미시랑은 하늘에 있는 미륵님이 직접 인간으로 오신 것이라 합니다. 이 미시랑이 인간 세상에서 7년 교화를 하고 어느 날 사라졌다는 것입니다.

this entity, asserting in school history texts that Jin's existence as a so-called 'state' or a group was just a conjecture.

Gyeongju, the capital of the Silla Dynasty, was a sacred place of Maitreya faith. Silla's Maitreya faith was proud and novel in some aspects. From where came the driving force to unify the Three Kingdoms and to set straight the foundation of Silla's Buddhist culture, which spanned almost one thousand years? Of course, the role of the Hwarang Knights was significant, but the crucial source of the driving force was the faith that in the future Maitreya Buddha, the Lord of Tushita Heaven, would come to this land to fundamentally reform this world and open a new one.

King Jinheung, who dreamed of becoming the "Wheel-turning Monarch,"* named his two sons Dongryun ("Copper Wheel") and Saryun ("House Wheel") respectively. Not only the Silla king but also King Seong, the twenty-sixth King

> **The Wheel-turning Monarch.** The Indian ideal of a universal monarch who rules the world using a wheel endowed upon him at his enthronement.

of Baekje, had an idea that he was the very Wheel-turning Monarch who would accomplish the ideal of Maitreya Buddha and build the Dragon Flower Paradise. In Japan, King Seong was called 'King Seong-myeong' ("Holy Virtue and Bright Wisdom"). Influenced by their deep Maitreya faith, the early Silla Dynasty produced a traditional song called "Dosolga" ("Song of Tushita"). Why was the song given such a title? Where did the faith in the Maitreya of Tushita Heaven originate from? It is truly mysterious. In Silla, a legend arose of a youth called 'Misi' who was renowned as an "immortal flower of Maitreya." According to the legend, he was Maitreya Buddha incarnate who had descended from heaven as a human, and he edified humanity for seven years before suddenly disappearing one day.

'신라 진지왕(재위 576~579) 때 흥륜사의 승려 진자眞慈가
미륵선화 미시랑 未尸郎을 만났는데 7년 뒤에 문득 간 곳이 없었다.'

(『삼국유사』「탑상塔像」)

그런데 바로 이 무렵 신라 천년 역사의 국력이 가장 강력하게 결집할 수 있는 화랑도 조직이 아주 빠르게 체계화되었습니다. 원광법사圓光法師가 이 때 등장해서 환국·배달·조선에서부터 내려온 그 소도 제천의 성지에서 우주광명의 인간 심법을 전수하는, 경당扃堂에서 가르친 오상지도五常之道를 바탕으로 해서 세속오계世俗五戒를 내려 주었습니다. '원광'은 우주광명이라는 뜻입니다. 원광법사가 중국에 유학을 했는데 학문이 얼마나 방대한지 유학에도 도통했습니다. 신라 왕가에서 이분을 모셔다가 모든 외교문서를 관장하게 했습니다. 원광법사는 백 살 가까이 되도록 살다가 세상을 떠났습니다.

원광법사 | 541~630
중국 수나라 유학. 도교와 유교를 회통

Dharma Master Wongwang (541 – 630).
▪ Studied in the Sui Dynasty of China.
▪ Erudite regarding Daoism and
  Confucianism.

"During the period of King Jinji of Silla (r. 576-579), Jinja, a Buddhist monk of Heungnyunsa Temple, met a youth called 'Misi,' who happened to be 'an immortal flower of Maitreya,' but suddenly he was nowhere to be seen seven years later."
(Source: "Pagodas and Buddhist Images" *Samguk Yusa*)

By the way, in approximately this era, the system of the Hwarang Knights swiftly became established, enabling the national power of Silla to reach its zenith during its history of almost one thousand years. Dharma Master Wongwang emerged around this time. At a *sodo*, a sacred site where heavenly rituals had been offered since the ancient eras of Hwanguk, Baedal, and Joseon, he conveyed the Five Commandments for Laymen based on the Five Constant Ways taught in *gyeongdang*s, schools for youth built next to *sodo*s. The Five Constant Ways had been taught to convey the mindset of humans of cosmic radiance. '*Wongwang*' means "cosmic radiance." Dharma Master Wongwang had studied in China and possessed such extensive learning that he was knowledgeable about even Confucianism. The Silla Dynasty assigned to him the task of preparing all diplomatic documents. He passed away just short of one hundred years of age.

청도 운문사 벽화 | 원광법사는 귀산貴山과 추항箒項 두 화랑에게 세속오계를 전했다. 600년(진평왕 22)

Mural at Unmunsa Temple in Cheongdo County
Dharma Master Wongwang conveyed the Five Commandments for Laymen to two leaders of the Hwarang Knights, Gwisan and Chuhang, in 600 CE (King Jinpyeong's twenty-second year of reign).

충忠, 효孝, 신信, 인仁, 용勇이라는 것은 유가에서 온 것이 아니라, 원광법사가 자기를 찾아온 두 젊은이 귀산貴山과 추항箒項에게 화랑의 계율로 내려 준 것입니다. 임금을 섬기되 충으로, 부모를 섬기되 효로, 친구를 사귀되 믿음으로 하라는 것입니다. 그리고 살생유택殺生有擇, 임전무퇴臨戰無退를 말했습니다.

환국 오상지도	화랑 세속오계
충忠	사군이충
효孝	사친이효
신信	교우이신
인仁	살생유택
용勇	임전무퇴

호국불교의 화랑도 정신은 정말로 강력한 것입니다. 김유신 장군은 전쟁에 나가는 자기 아들에게 목숨을 걸고 싸우라고 했는데, 패하고 살아서 돌아왔다고, 그 아들을 인간으로 여기지도 않고 부모가 평생 만나지 않았습니다. 그 아들은 산속에 들어가서 숨어 살다가 죽었잖아요. 신라에는 이처럼 감동적인 화랑 문화가 있었습니다.

The five ways of loyalty, filial piety, faith, benevolence, and bravery were not from Confucianism, but were given by Dharma Master Wongwang to two young men, named Gwisan and Chuhang, who had come to see him, as commandments for the Hwarang Knights. According to these commandments, one should: serve the king with loyalty, serve one's parents with filial piety, make friends with faith, be discriminating about the taking of life, and never retreat on the battlefield.

Hwanguk: The Five Constant Ways	The Hwarang Knights: The Five Commandments for Laymen
Loyalty	Serve the king with loyalty.
Filial Piety	Serve one's parents with filial piety.
Faith	Make friends with faith.
Benevolence	Be discriminating about the taking of life.
Bravery	Never retreat on the battlefield.

Based on "nation-protecting Buddhism," the spirit of the Hwarang Knights was truly strong. General Gim Yusin, [a leader of the Hwarang Knights when young,] ordered his son, also a leader of the Hwarang Knights, to fight at the risk of his life when the latter headed for battle, but his son ended up coming back alive after being defeated. Considering him a disgrace to the family, Gim Yusin and his wife refused to ever see him again. The son hid in a mountain for the rest of his life. Silla had just such an inspiring culture in the form of the Hwarang Knights.

신라 역사·문화의 원형정신

신라 역사문화의 원형정신은 무엇인가? 이제 신라 역사문화의 원형정신을 살펴보기로 하겠습니다.

천년 신라의 원형문화, 소도제천

신라 6촌의 장들이 살았던 지역 이름 속에 신라 역사문화를 만든 원형정신, 문화의 근원정신이 그대로 살아있습니다.

신채호는 "박혁거세는 6부의 총왕總王"이라는 재미있는 표현을 쓰고 있습니다.

Chapter 2

The Original Spirit of Silla's History and Culture

What is the original spirit of Silla's history and culture? Now, let us examine it.

The Original Culture of Silla's Thousand-Year-Long History : Offering Heavenly Rituals at Sodos

The original spirit of Silla's history, or the root spirit of Silla's culture, lives onward in the names of the regions where the heads of the six villages lived.

Eminent Korean historian Sin Chao-ho used an interesting expression: "Bak Hyeokgeose was the overall king of six regions."

The foster father who raised Bak Hyeokgeose was Sobeoldori of Goheochon Village. The group with the clan name 'So' that originated from the Jinju region asserts that Sobeoldori was their ancestor. Close examination of the genealogy of the So Clan from Jinju shows that they likely can be traced back to Hwanguk. Is it not amazing that the So Clan came from Hwanguk?

박혁거세朴赫居世를 길러 주신 수양아버지가 고허촌高墟村의 소벌도리蘇伐都利입니다. 지금 진주 소씨晉州蘇氏도 '소벌도리가 우리 조상'이라 합니다. 진주 소씨의 족보를 이번에 체계적으로 보니까, 환국에서 발원이 됐습니다. 소씨는 환국에서 왔다는 것입니다. 놀랍지 않아요?

소씨는 환국에서 왔고, 그 후손 가운데서 소벌도리가 나왔다는 이야기가 있습니다. 태하공太夏公 69세손 진공辰公 백손伯孫이 남쪽 경주로 왔는데 고허촌 촌장 소벌蘇伐이 진공의 현손이라 합니다.

적제赤帝   진주 소씨의 시조, 환국의 왕
 ↓
백손伯孫   적제의 129세손 → 경주에서 후진한의 왕이 됨
 ↓
소벌도리   적제의 133세손: 고허촌장

(『진주 소씨 부소보서』)

제가 경주 최씨慶州崔氏한테 물어봤습니다. 그랬더니 경주 최씨의 뿌리는 최치원이고 최치원의 뿌리는 소벌도리라는 것입니다. 진주 소씨와 경주 최씨 두 성씨의 뿌리는 소벌도리공입니다.

그런데 6촌의 뜻을 보면 신라의 역사문화가 어떻게 탄생됐는지 알 수 있습니다.

6촌명	성씨	시조
알천 양산촌	이씨	알평
돌산 고허촌	최씨·소씨	소벌도리
무산 대수촌	손씨	구례마
취산 진지촌	정씨	지백호
금산 가리촌	배씨	지타
명활산 고야촌	설씨	호진

Furthermore, in regards to the possibility that the So Clan originated from Hwanguk and that Sobeoldori was their descendant, Duke Tae-ha's sixty-ninth generation descendant, Baekson, Lord of Jin, is said to have relocated southward—that is, to Gyeongju—and the head of Go-heochon Village, Sobeoldori, was the Lord of Jin's great-great-grandson.

Red Emperor	The progenitor of the So Clan from the Jinju region. A monarch of Hwanguk.
Baekson	The Red Emperor's 129th descendant, he became a king of Later Jinhan in Gyeongju.
Sobeoldori	The Red Emperor's 133rd descendant, he was head of Goheochon Village.

(Source: Preface to *The Genealogy of the So Clan from Jinju*)

I questioned a member of the Choe Clan from Gyeongju, and he said that they derived from Choe Chiwon and that Choe Chiwon's origin was Sobeoldori. The root of both clans, the So Clan from the Jinju region and the Choe Clan from the Gyeongju region, was Sobeoldori.

An examination of the meaning of the names of Silla's original six villages reveals how the culture of Silla was established.

Village Name	Clan Name	Progenitor
Yangsanchon in Alcheon	Yi	Alpyeong
Goheochon in Dolsan	Choe and So	Sobeoldori
Daesuchon in Musan	Son	Guryema
Jinjichon in Jasan (or Chwisan)	Jeong	Jibaekho
Garichon in Geumsan	Bae	Jita
Goyachon in Myeonghwalsan	Seol	Hojin

예를 들어서 알천關川 양산촌楊山村을 보면, 양산은 버드나무 당목이 있는 당산촌, 솟터입니다. 돌산突山 고허촌高墟村은 높은 터, 솟은 터니까 소도蘇塗입니다. 그 다음 무산茂山 대수촌大樹村을 보면, 대수는 글자 그대로 큰 나무, 소도입니다.

동서양에 성상聖像 문화가 있는데, 러시아에 가면 이콘icon 문화가 있습니다. 인형을 재미있게 깎아서 길에서 파는 모스크바의 시장에 가보면 이콘 문화를 볼 수 있습니다.

동서고금의 모든 이콘 문화의 뿌리는 바로 6천 년 전에 환국 우주광명 문화 역사를 가지고 백두산에 오셔서 신시에 터를 잡으신 환웅을 섬긴 일입니다. 『산해경山海經』을 보면 큰 산 속에 있는 가장 큰 나무를 환웅님의 성령이 항상 임재해 계신다는 신성한 나무, '웅상雄像'으로 받들었습니다.

알천 양산촌楊山村	돌산 고허촌高墟村	무산 대수촌大樹村
• 버들(楊)은 당목堂木의 한 종류 • 당산촌堂山村	• 高(솟다) 墟(터) → 솟터(소도)	• 大(큰) 樹(나무) → 솟대(소도)

자산 진지촌珍支村	금산 가리촌加利村	명활산 고야촌高耶村
• 珍(보배) 支(괴다, 지탱하다) → 솟대	• 가리加利는 솟는 단=대가리(大神) → 큰 신을 모시는 성지(소도)	• 고야高耶 → 솟은 곳

Speaking of Yangsanchon Village in Alcheon, the name 'Yangsan' signifies a hill in a village, where a willow tree was planted as a village deity [*Yang* and *san* mean "willow" and "hill" respectively; *chon* means "village"]. The name 'Goheo' in 'Goheochon Village' denotes an elevated site and signifies a *sodo*. 'Daesu' in 'Daesuchon' literally means "big tree" and signifies a *sodo*.

The tradition of iconolatry exists in both the East and the West. In Russia, they also have a tradition of iconolatry, and we glimpse this in Moscow markets where interesting-looking carved wooden dolls are sold.

The origin of all iconolatry in the East and West was the practice of worshipping Hwanung, who brought from Hwanguk the culture of cosmic radiance and settled in Sinsi ("Divine City") of Mt. Baekdusan about six thousand years ago. According to the *Classic of Mountains and Seas*, people in the East worshiped the tallest tree on a big mountain as a sacred tree, an '*ungsang*,' in which Hwanung's holy spirit was always present.

Yangsanchon Village in Alcheon	A willow served as a deity tree in this village. It was a village with a hill on which the village deity tree was located.
Goheochon Village in Dolsan	*Go* (means "elevated" or "high"), and *heo* ("site") signifies "elevated site" (or a *sodo*).
Daesuchon Village in Musan	*Dae* ("big") plus *su* ("tree") signifies a sacred pole (or a *sodo*).
Jinjichon Village in Jasan	*Jin* ("treasure") plus *ji* ("prop up") signifies a sacred pole.
Garichon Village in Geumsan	A *gari* (an elevated altar) is also called a '*daegari*' ("great deity") and signifies a *sodo* or a sacred place for worshipping a great deity.
Goyachon Village in Myeonghwalsan	'*Goya*' signifies an elevated ground.

이것이 일본에 전해져서 산 자체를 신체神體, 신의 몸으로 숭배합니다. 대국주신大國主神을 모신 아주 유명한 사찰, 일본 역사의 근원, 시원을 말하는 바로 오오미와(大神) 신사가 그렇습니다.

신라 6촌 가운데 대수촌에는 환웅천황을 모신 웅상처럼 신수를 모시는 문화가 그대로 나타나 있습니다.

그다음 자산觜山의 진지촌珍支村인데 자觜라는 것은 동방 천자문화를 상징합니다. 진지촌은 보배 진珍 자에 괴다, 지탱하다는 뜻의 지支 자를 썼으니 이 진지는 솟대라는 말입니다. 또 금산金山의 가리촌加利村에서 '가리'라는 것은 솟은 단을 상징하고, 대신大神을 뜻합니다. 가리를 대가리大嘉利라고도 합니다. 그러니까 가리는 큰 신을 모시는 성지, 소도입니다. 그리고 명활산明活山의 고야촌高耶村에서 '고야'는 솟은 곳, 솟터입니다.

소도라는 것은 환국, 배달, 조선의 문화 창조의 중심지입니다. 인류의 모든 문화는 어디서 나왔는가?

지금 6촌장들이 자리 잡은 어떤 특정한 성스러운 공간에서 보듯이 이 솟터에서 나왔습니다. 인류 역사문화는 솟터, 소도에서 나왔습니다.

소도蘇塗라는 말에서, 소蘇라는 것은 끊임없이 소생한다, 솟구친다는 뜻입니다. 끊임없이 새로운 우주의 광명, 신성한 생명이 솟구치는 것입니다. 도塗라는 것은 터라는 뜻입니다. 소도문화의 원형은 환웅천황을 모시는 웅상문화입니다.

This practice was transmitted to Japan, where people began to worship mountains as the body of a deity. The famous Ōmiwa Shrine is an example. That shrine is dedicated to *Ōkuninushi-no-Kami* ("Master of the Great Land"), and the shrine also reveals the root of Japanese history.

In Daesuchon Village, one of Silla's six original villages, appeared the tradition of worshipping a sacred tree, a practice similar to worshipping *ungsang*s, a symbol of Heavenly Emperor Hwanung.

In the case of Jinjichon Village in Jasan, the character *ja* (觜) in 'Jasan' symbolizes the Eastern culture of the Son of Heaven (and *san* means "mountain" or "hill"). The name 'Jinjichon' consists of the characters *jin* ("treasure"), *ji* ("prop up" or "support"), and *chon* ("village"), and, combined, '*jinji*' signifies a sacred pole. Concerning the name 'Garichon,' *gari* symbolizes both an elevated altar and a great deity. A *gari* is also called a '*daegari*' (*dae* means "great"). Thus, '*gari*' signifies a *sodo* or a sacred site where a great deity is worshipped. In the name 'Goyachon Village,' *goya* signifies an elevated site.

A *sodo* was the center of the creation of cultures during the eras of Hwanguk, Baedal, and Joseon. By the way, from where did all the cultures of humanity originate? As we can see in the cases of certain sacred places where the heads of Silla's six villages settled, humanity's cultures originated from 'elevated sites' or *sodo*s.

In the name '*sodo*,' *so* signifies "to endlessly revive" or "surge." That is, new cosmic radiance or sacred life energy endlessly erupts. *Do* signifies a ground or a site. The origin of *sodo* culture was the practice of worshipping *ungsang*, during which Heavenly Emperor Hwanung was worshipped.

이것을 대중화한 분은 단군조선의 11세 도해道奚단군입니다. 그때 열두 개의 아주 잘 생긴 성상을 선택해서 열두 소도 터를 닦았습니다. 영고탑寧古塔은 소도 제천단이 있던 곳입니다.

단군왕검 시절 9년 홍수로 중국 역사가 무너지려고 할 때, 부루 태자가 산동성에 있는 낭야성에 갔습니다. 지금도 중국에서 낭야성을 그대로 보존하고 있습니다. 거기에 가서 순임금에게 9년 홍수의 참담한 역사현장 이야기를 보고 받고, 경당局堂을 세우고 이 소도 제천 문화를 크게 부흥시키라는 명을 내렸습니다.

그 뒤에 주周나라를 창건할 때 정승 노릇을 한, 문왕과 무왕을 보필한 강태공姜太公이 팔신제八神祭라는 체계를 가지고 소도문화를 중국에 크게 퍼뜨리게 됩니다.

낭야대 | 산동성 교남시
Nangya Platform, Jiaonan City, Shandong Province

The one who made *sodo*s widely available to people was Dangun Dohae, Joseon's eleventh ruler. He had twelve objects with striking appearances selected as icons and established twelve *sodo* sites for them. Yeonggotap was a place where a *sodo* with an altar for heavenly rituals was located.

When Dangun Wanggeom was ruling Joseon, China was facing collapse due to the flood that had plagued it for nine years. Crown Prince Buru of Joseon went to Nangya-seong Fortress in Shandong Province. The fortress is still preserved today. There, King Shun of China reported the disastrous status of the nine-year flood to Crown Prince Buru. Crown Prince Buru ordered King Shun to build schools called '*gyeong-dangs*' for youth next to *sodo*s and to widely establish the custom of offering heavenly rituals at *sodo*s.

Later, Grand Duke Gang (aka, 'Jiang Ziya'), who had assisted King Wen and King Wu of the Zhou Dynasty in the initial stage of its foundation, serving as a minister, widely established in China the custom of establishing *sodo*s and offering heavenly rituals there, through the practice of offering heavenly rituals to eight deities.

부루태자 | Crown Prince Buru

순임금 | King Shun

중국의 9년 대홍수를 해결한 단군왕검의 아들 부루태자 | Dangun Wanggeom's son, Crown Prince Buru, solved the great flood that plagued China for nine years.

야쿠츠크 축제 솟대 | 러시아 사하공화국
Sacred poles in Yakutsk festival – Sakha Republic, Russia

한국의 솟대 신앙 |
The practice of worshipping sacred poles in Korea

오벨리스크 | 튀르키예 이스탄불 히포드롬광장
Obelisk - Hippodrome Square, Istanbul, Turkey

The Original Spirit of Silla's History and Culture 135

소도에서 삼신을 모시는 제관이 삼랑三郞입니다. 강화도에는 마리산 참성단 주변에 삼랑성이 있습니다. 바로 이 소도에서 삼신을 수호하는 관직이 삼랑이고, 이 삼랑문화를 계승한 것이 화랑입니다. 삼랑에서 화랑이 나왔습니다.

The ritual officials who served Samsin at *sodo*s were the Samnang. On Ganghwa-do Island, near Mt. Marisan's Chamseongdan Altar, is located a fortress called 'Samnang-seong.' The Hwarang Knights in Silla succeeded the tradition of the Samnang, the officials who guarded Samsin at the *sodo*s. That is, the root of the Hwarang Knights was the Samnang.

강화도 삼랑성三郞城 |
Samnang-seong Fortress in Ganghwa-do Island

단군조선 때는 천지화天指花, 하늘에서 지적해 준 꽃을 꽂고 다녔습니다. 그래서 천지화랑天指花郎입니다. 신라에서는 남모와 준정 두 아가씨를 데려다가 원화源花로 길렀는데 준정이 남모에게 술을 먹여서 강물에 빠뜨려 죽였습니다. 그래서 원화를 폐지하고, 10대 소년 중에서 인간성이 좋고 용기와 의리가 있는 자를 추천 받아서 제도화, 조직화한 것이 화랑입니다. 그 책임자를 풍월주風月主라 합니다.

이 소도의 문화 사상은 실제 어디서 완성되는가? 소도에는 반드시 경당扃堂이 있었습니다. 경당은 인류 학교 문화의 고향이에요. 동서양의 모든 학교, 대학이라는 건 경당에서 온 것입니다.

경당扃이라는 것은 공경한다는 경敬 자하고 통합니다. 그러니까 경당은 공경하는 마음을 길러주는 집입니다. 모든 생명의 근원은 바로 삼신입니다. 삼신의 사기현현自己顯現이 하늘과 땅과 인간입니다. 인간은 피소물物이 아니라는 것입니다. 인간은 이 대우주 창조 생명, 그 영원한 우주광명의 존재 자체입니다.

그래서 우주 원형 역사문화의 근본정신을 전해 주는, 그 우주광명의 심법을 전해 주는 그 문화 탄생의 공부방이 경당입니다. 경扃은 밝을 경으로도 쓰는데 고전에 보면 '아심我心이 경경扃扃'(『춘추좌씨전』), 내 마음이 밝고 밝다는 말이 있습니다.

In the era of Dangun Joseon, elite youths wore in their hair *cheonjihwa* ("flower designated by heaven"), and thus were called 'Cheonji Hwarang' (*cheonjihwa* plus *rang* ["man" or "youth"]). In Silla, two young women, Nammo and Junjeong, were originally designated as the leaders (with the title of *wonhwa*, "original flower") of two divided groups of elite youths. The two women were in stiff competition with each other, and that competition culminated with Junjeong's killing of Nammo, by luring her into getting drunk and throwing her into a river. As a result, the practice of having young women as leaders was abolished. Instead, only male teenagers with good character, courage, and fidelity were accepted into the newly established Hwarang Knights. The leader of the group was titled the 'Master of Wind and Moon.'

By the way, what was the ultimate result of the tradition of *sodo*s? Actually, every *sodo* had attached schools called 'gyeongdangs,' and *gyeongdang*s were the root of all of humanity's schools. Therefore, all schools, including universities, both in the East and West, originated from this concept of the *gyeongdang*.

The character *gyeong* (扃, "to look closely") in 'gyeongdang' is related to the character *gyeong* (敬, "to respect") [and *dang*, meaning "a house"]. Therefore, the term 'gyeongdang' signifies a house where a respectful mindset is cultivated. The origin of all beings is none other than Samsin. The self manifestation of Samsin is heaven, earth, and humanity. So, humanity are not creatures, but rather the creative life energy of this great universe, or the eternal cosmic radiance itself. Thus, a *gyeongdang* was a study room wherein cultures are born—where the fundamental spirit of the universe's primordial history and culture or the mindset of cosmic radiance was transmitted. The character *gyeong* (扃, "to look closely") can also mean "to be bright" as in the following phrase from a classic titled *Zuo Zhuan* : (我心扃扃) "my mind is bright and bright."

이 경당에서 배우는 학동, 도생을 국자랑國子郞이라 합니다. 『단군세기』에 보면, 환웅이 3천 명 개척단을 데리고 왔는데 그 정신을 계승한 것이 바로 이 국자랑입니다. 이 국자랑을 계승한 것이 북부여의 천왕랑天王郞입니다. 그것이 신라의 화랑으로 내려왔습니다. 고구려는 검은 옷을 입고 띠를 두르고서 조의선인皂衣仙人이라 했습니다. 이 조의선인 문화가 일본에 그대로 가 있습니다.

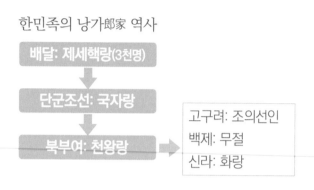

한민족의 낭가郞家 역사

배달: 제세핵랑(3천명)

↓

단군조선: 국자랑

↓

북부여: 천왕랑 →

고구려: 조의선인
백제: 무절
신라: 화랑

일본의 소도 문화

인류의 문화는 솟터에서 탄생했습니다. 솟터를 상징하는, 아주 재미있는 것이 뭐예요? 바로 솟터에 세우는 솟대입니다. 일본 신사 앞에 세 개씩 도리이(鳥居)를 세웁니다. 경주 삼랑사지三郞寺址 당간지주幢竿支柱도 솟터에 세우는 일종의 솟대와 같습니다.

The students who studied in *gyeongdang*s were called 'Gukjarang.' According to *Dangun Segi*, Hwanung brought three thousand pioneers with him, and their mindset endured in the later Gukjarang. Gukjarang was then succeeded by the Cheonwangnang of Northern Buyeo. In Silla, the tradition was inherited by the Hwarang Knights. In the case of Goguryeo, there was a group called 'Jo-uiseonin,' whose members wore black attire and belts. The institution of Jo-uiseonin was transmitted to Japan, where it went through little change.

The succession of *nang*s in the Korean nation's history.

Baedal: Jesehaengnang (3,000 members)

↓

Dangun Joseon: Gukjarang

↓

Northern Buyeo: Cheonwangnang →

Goguryeo: Jo-uiseonin
Baekje: Mujeol
Silla: Hwarang Knights

Sodo Culture in Japanese Shrines

Humanity's culture in general started from elevated sites. What is an interesting symbol of such sites? It is the sacred poles erected on those sites. The gateways of three *torii* erected in front of Japanese Shinto shrines and the flagpole supports in the Samnangsa Temple site in Gyeongju are all forms of sacred poles built on elevated sites.

당간(깃대)을 고정하던 두 기둥(좌), 경주 삼랑사지 당간지주(우) |
Two columns to fasten a flagpole (left)
Flagpole support at Samnangsa Temple site, Gyeongju
(right)

우리가 일본으로 전수된 솟터 문화를 잠깐 보면, 일본 신사 속에 소도문화가 그대로 있습니다. 동경에 있는 아사쿠사(淺草) 또는 센소지(淺草寺)를 가보면 지구 창세 문화의 원형 소도문화가 그대로 전수된 것을 알 수 있습니다.

일본에서 명치유신 이후에 내린 특명이 무엇입니까? 조선에서 내려온 사찰이라든지 신사는 다 축소하든지 없애라는 신불분리령神佛分離令이 내려졌습니다. 신사와 불당이 한 울타리에 있었는데 이것을 떼어 놓고 없애는 겁니다. 그 대표적인 것이 이름이 변경되고 약화된 도쿄 아사쿠사입니다. 아사쿠사에 가보면, 그 원형을 누구도 못 찾습니다.

물 낮을 천淺 자에다 풀 초草 자를 썼습니다. 천박하게 천초신사淺草神社, 천초사淺草寺라고 '물 얕은 데에서 풀이 나왔다'고 하는 것입니다.

센소지의 한자 음	물얕을 천
Cheoncho: Hanja pronunciation of 'Senso-ji'	淺 *cheon* ("shallow water")
	풀 초
	草 *cho* ("grass")

센소지淺草寺 ǀ 동경 아사쿠사   Senso-ji Temple in Asakusa, Tokyo

By examining the practice of erecting sacred poles, which was transmitted to Japan, we can find the *sodo* culture in Japanese Shinto shrines. A visit to Senso-ji Temple in Asakusa Tokyo testifies to the transmission of the original form of the *sodo*-establishing tradition from the world's first culture.

What was the special order that Japanese people received when the Meiji Restoration began? It was to separate Shinto shrines and Buddhist temples that had coexisted in the same precincts until that point. Under the order, Buddhist temples or Shinto shrines associated with Joseon were to be either reduced or removed. One typical example that went through a change of this sort was Asakusa Shrine in Tokyo, which was renamed and demeaned. Its original form is nowhere to be seen. The temple name in the area uses the characters *cheon* (浅 "shallow water") and *cho* (草 "grass"); and when combined, the name means "Grass comes from shallow water," which is not a dignified name.

삼신三神이 타는 세 대의 가마 | 동경 센소지
Three sedan chairs in which three spirits ride. (Senso-ji Temple in Tokyo).

여기에 '비불祕佛'이라 해서 도래인渡來人들이 바다에 빠뜨린 부처를 건져 내어서 숨겨놓고 있습니다.

그런데 거기 앞에 입구에 가보면 역사 비밀이 쭉 써져 있는데, 거기에 뭐가 있는가? 마지막 간판에, 바로 칠복신七福神* 신앙을 한다는 것입니다. '일곱 가지 복을 가지고 들어온다'는 것은 기독교에서 말하는 일곱 성령의 은혜, 칠복사상과 통하는 것이 있습니다.

아사쿠사는 무엇인가? 그 안내문을 쭉 보고서 아사쿠사는 아사달이 변형된 것이라고 제가 정리를 해 줬습니다. 아사쿠사는 아사달입니다.

칠복신七福神(시치후쿠신)
①에비스惠比寿
②다이코쿠텡大黒天
③벤자이텡弁財天
④비샤몬텡毘沙門天
⑤후쿠로쿠쥬福禄寿
⑥쥬로오징寿老人
⑦호테에布袋

Sanja Festival ("Three Shrine Festival") of Asakusa Shrine
→ Three spirits are brought into the temple.

In this temple, a "secret Buddha" is concealed—a Buddha statue that migrants from Korea dropped in the sea and that was later retrieved by the people. On the information boards at the entrance of the temple is revealed a historical secret. What is this secret? The last board reads: "In this temple, they practice faith in the Seven Lucky Gods."* The thought that the Seven Gods bring 'seven fortune' is somewhat connected to the blessings of God's seven spirits mentioned in Christianity.

What does the name 'Asakusa' mean? After reading the information boards, I came to the conclusion that 'Asakusa' is a modified form of the name 'Asadal.' That is, 'Asakusa' is basically the same as 'Asadal.'

Seven Lucky Gods. Ebisu: the god of fishermen and merchants. Daikokuten: the god of wealth, commerce, and trade. Benzaiten: the goddess of knowledge, art, and beauty. Bishamonten: the god of warriors and defence against evil. Fukurokuju: the god of happiness, wealth, and longevity. Jurōjin: the god of wisdom and long life. Hotei: the god of abundance and good health.

Japanese faith in the Seven Lucky Gods

그 옆에 들어갈 때 오른쪽에 있는 신사가 센소지 절인데, 거기서 동경의 3대 마츠리 중 하나를 하는데 외국 사람도 엄청나게 많이 온다고 합니다. 그런데 이 센소지에서 세 신을 모셔오는 마츠리를 합니다. 아사쿠사는 삼신·칠성 신앙이 정착한 소도의 땅입니다.

그런데 이 지역을 나오면서 보면 지역을 먹여 살리는 재벌 회사가 하나 있습니다. 저 유명한, 우리 동네에도 마실 수 있는 아사히 맥주 공장이 있습니다. 아사히(朝日)는 무엇인가? 아사달입니다. '히'라는 것은 해니까 '아침 해'입니다. 그래서 그 회사가 안 망합니다. 1980년대에 불황이 와서 부도날 위기에 있었는데, 아사히라는 걸 영어로 멋있게 디자인했더니 '아사히, 아사히' 하고 일본에서 난리가 났습니다. 지금 저 오른쪽 대형 건물에 황금 색깔로 맥주 공장 로고를 저렇게 만들어 놨습니다.

아사히
(朝日, 아침 해)   ← 단군조선의 수도
아사달에서 유래

Asahi
"Morning Sun"   ← The name 'Asahi' originated from the capital of Dangun Joseon, Asadal.

아사히맥주 본사 전경 | 일본 동경
Asahi Beer headquarters, Tokyo, Japan

The shrine on the right is Senso-ji Buddhist Temple, where one of three major festivals in Tokyo is held, attracting a huge number of foreign tourists too, they say. At this festival, three spirits are brought into the temple. Asakusa Shrine was a *sodo* site where the faiths in Samsin ("Three Spirits") and in the Seven Stars took root.

If one tours this region before leaving it, they will notice large buildings belonging to the famous Asahi Beer company that sustains this region. Their beer is available even in our neighborhood. What is 'Asahi' (朝日)? It is 'Asadal.' The *hi* in 'Asahi' means "the sun" [and *asa* means "morning"], so 'Asahi' means "Morning Sun." Thanks to the power of its name, the company is not likely to go out of business easily. In fact, it was once in danger of bankruptcy in the 1980s, hit by a business recession. What they did then was to change their company logo into a stylish English form, which gained great popularity in Japan. On the big building on the right side [of the photo] is displayed a golden logo of the company.

우리가 이즈모 대사를 가보면, 신라에서 내려간 그 역사의 조상들과 연관돼 있음을 알 수 있습니다. 이 신사 신락전神樂殿에 가보면 거대한 금줄이 있습니다. 이 이즈모의 신사의 원형은 피라미드 구조로 아래에서 위로 계단을 따라서 올라가는 모습입니다.

저 신락전 기둥이 얼마나 거대한지 아무리 팔이 긴 사람도 저것을 끌어안을 수가 없습니다. 그런 큰 기둥 세 개를 하나로 엮어서, 아홉 개를 세웠습니다.

이 우주 삼신문화, 삼신일체 사상, 3수 사상의 종합판이 이즈모의 초기 신사의 기둥인데, 그 모형을 저렇게 한쪽에 세워 놓고 있습니다.

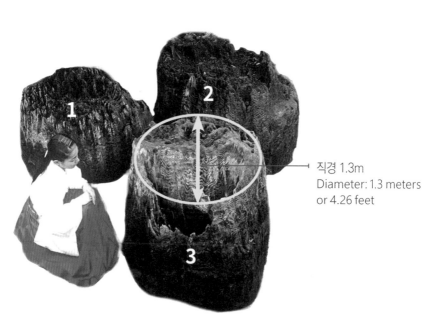

직경 1.3m
Diameter: 1.3 meters
or 4.26 feet

기둥 3개를 하나로 묶어서 사용 → 삼신일체 사상을 보여줌
Three columns were bound together and stood as one. They represented the concept of the One God who impels all existence via three means.

Izumo Grand Shrine is noticeably related to the history of the people who migrated from Silla. A huge straw rope (to ward off evil spirits) is hung in the shrine compound's Kagura Hall. The original form of the shrine was a pyramid structure to whose top people ascended by stairs.

The columns of Kagura Hall are so huge that nobody, not even a person with long arms, can encompass one with their arms. Earlier, those three columns were bound together and stood as one, and nine such columns were built. The columns of Izumo Grand Shrine's original form are a good example of the integration of: the tradition of worshipping Samsin, the concept of One God who impels all existence via three means; with the concept of valuing the number "three." A replica of the columns is displayed on one side.

복원한 기둥 모형
A replica of the
reconstructed columns

신전
The Shrine

신락전神樂殿의 금줄 | 이즈모대사
The huge straw rope of Kagura Hall in Izumo Grand Shrine

이즈모대사 원형 복원도
A reconstruction of Izumo Grand Shrine's original form

신라의 역사가 탄생한 비밀이 6촌장의 소도문화에 있고 소도문화에는 경당이 있었고, 그리고 바로 거기에서 우주광명의 심법을 전수받는 것을 상징하는, 솟대를 세우는 예식이 있었습니다.

신라 소도문화의 진실

일본의 스와신사에서 만 6년 만에 한 번씩 네 개의 신사에서 각각 네 개씩 열여섯 개의 신성한 나무, 솟대를 세우는데 그 솟대에 담겨 있는 역사 비밀은 과연 무엇인가?

신라 소도 제천문화의 왜곡과 잘못된 이해, 소도문화에 대한 진실을 바로잡으면서 이 우주 원형 문화 역사의 비밀을 한번 총체적으로 단숨에 풀어보기로 하겠습니다.

우물 정# 자는 시원 문화의 비밀입니다. 이것을 잘못 이해하고 있기 때문에 신라 역사문화의 근원, 문화 원형정신을 오해하고 있습니다. 단순한 우물 정이 아닙니다.

자, 시조 박혁거세가 탄생한 나정羅#으로 가볼까요? 나정은 남산 아래쪽에 있는데, 저기 중앙에 올라가서 서봐야 나정의 수수께끼가 내 가슴에 들어옵니다. 나정은 너무도 잘못 알려졌습니다. 저기 발굴 초기 모습을 보면 어떻게 되어 있나요? 저 중앙이 지금은 원형으로 되어 있는데, 거기만 닭이 알을 품고 있는 것처럼 천연적으로 높습니다. 그런데 그것이 본래 발굴을 할 때 팔각으로 되어 있었다는 것입니다. 그러면 이 팔각이 뭘 의미하는가? 나정에는 그동안 '우물이 있었다'고 하지만, 우물이 아니라 그 터에는 어떤 기둥이 박혀 있던 흔적이 있더라는 것입니다.

The key to the Silla Dynasty's birth can be found in the custom of establishing *sodo*s in the six villages. Wherever a *sodo* was, there was a school called a '*gyeongdang*' next to it. They performed a ritual of erecting sacred poles at *gyeongdang*s as a symbolic act of inheriting the mindset of cosmic radiance.

The Truth About Silla's Sodo Culture

Once every six years, in the Suwa Grand Shrine of Japan, people erect four sacred poles in each of the four shrines in the compound, raising sixteen of them in total. What is the historical secret of those sacred poles? To correct the distortion and false understandings of the Silla Dynasty's practice of establishing *sodo*s and offering heavenly rituals at these *sodo*s, and to convey the truth about *sodo*s, let me comprehensively explain the secret of this primordial culture at once.

The character *jeong* ("well") is a secret of the primordial culture. An incorrect understanding of this character leads one to misunderstand the origin of Silla's history and the fundamental spirit of its culture. The character *jeong* ("well") does not signify just any well. Now, shall we consider Najeong, where Silla's progenitor Bak Hyeokgeose was born? Najeong is located at the foot of Mt. Namsan. Only when you stand in the center of the site can you clearly decipher the riddle of Najeong. Najeong has been excessively misunderstood. What did it look like in its initial stage of excavation? Currently, the center of the site is round, and that center is naturally higher than other parts of the site, reminiscent of a brooding hen. However, when the site was first excavated, the center was said to have had an octagonal shape. Then what does the octagonal shape imply? Although it has been said that there was a well in Najeong, the traces of an embeded pillar were found instead of a well.

나정의 팔각 건물 터 발굴 모습 | 2002~2005
The excavation (2002 – 2005) of the remnants of an octagonal building site in Najeong

나정蘿井 | 신라 시조 박혁거세의 탄생지
Najeong: The birthplace of Bak Hyeokgeose, the progenitor of Silla

기존 우물터 |
The site of a presumed well.

팔각 건물의 기둥이 박혔던 자리로 확인됨
This turned out to be the site of embedded pillars for an octagonal building.

새로 발굴된 우물 터
The site of a newly excavated well

다음에, 알영정闕英井은 박혁거세의 왕비가 태어난 곳입니다.

다음으로 포석정鮑石亭을 가볼까요?

포석정은 신라의 경애왕景哀王이 술잔치를 벌이다가 견훤甄萱에게 공격을
받아서 자살한 곳이라는 수치스러운 망국의 한이 남아 있는 유적지인데 그
걸 사적 제1호로 정했습니다. 국보 1호 남대문, 보물 1호 동대문, 그 다음
에 사적 1호 포석정은 역사 왜곡의 대표적인 예입니다.

알영정闕英井 | 박혁거세 왕비의 탄생지
Alyeongjeong: The birthplace of Bak Hyeokgeose's queen

Next, Alyeongjeong was the birthplace of Bak Hyeokgeose's queen.

Next, shall we turn our attention to Poseokjeong?

Poseokjeong was a relic of disgrace due to the dynastic ruination that occurred when King Gyeongae, is said to have committed suicide when attacked militarily by Gyeon Hwon during a banquet. Poseokjeong was designated Historical Site No. 1. National Treasure No. 1, the Sungnyemun Gate (aka, 'South Gate'); Treasure No. 1, Heung-inmun Gate (aka, 'East Gate'); and Historical Site No. 1, Poseokjeong—these are all typical examples of historical distortion.

포석정鮑石亭 | 사적 제1호
Poseokjeong (Historical Site No.1)

일제의 문화재 등급을 답습한 한국의 문화재보호법(1962년)

일제		대한민국	제1호
보물	↗ ↘	국보	남대문
		보물	동대문
고적	→	사적	포석정

포석정은 원래 술판 벌이고 노는 곳이 아니라, 『화랑세기花郎世紀』 기록에도 포석사飽石祠로 되어 있습니다. 여기서 천제를 올렸고, 김춘추와 김유신의 동생 문희가 결혼을 했습니다. 그리고 가장 정의롭고 의기가 강한 화랑의 화신, 8대 풍월주風月主 문노文努를 여기에다 모셨습니다.

화랑세기가 전하는 포석사

1. 천제를 올린 신성한 장소
2. 김춘추와 문희(김유신 동생)의 혼례 장소
3. 제8대 화랑 문노文努의 화상을 모신 곳

그런데 이 포석정에 물이 내려가는 모양으로 해 놓은 유적의 형상은 하늘에 있는 천원, 하늘 정원 별자리를 모방하여 그대로 따놓은 것입니다. 이 얼마나 역사상 멋있는 유적인가요.

이 포석정 옆에는 남산에서 물이 아래쪽으로 내려오는데, 지금은 그 위에 보를 막아서 동네에서 물을 끌어쓰니까 물이 안 내려옵니다. 옛날에는 바위를 덮을 정도로 물이 힘차게 많이 흘렀을 것입니다. 그래서 왕족들이 거기서 목욕재계를 하고 길례吉禮를 올렸습니다. 국가 안녕을 위해서 기도를 한 것입니다.

The Cultural Property Protection Law of Korea (1962) followed the Cultural Property Classifications of Japanese imperialism.

Japanese Imperialism	Korea	No.1
Treasure	National Treasure	Sungnyemun Gate (aka, 'South Gate')
	Treasure	Heung-inmun Gate (aka, 'East Gate')
Ancient Site →	Historical Site	Poseokjeong

Originally, Poseokjeong was not a place for banquets: it was recorded as 'Poseoksa Shrine' in *Hwarang Segi*. In that shrine, heavenly rituals were offered, and Gim Chunchu and Gim Yusin's younger sister, Munhi, were married there. In addition, Munno, who was an embodiment of the most righteous and courageous Hwarang Knights and the eighth leader of the group, was enshrined there.

Poseoksa Shrine according to *Hwarang Segi*'s records:

1. A sacred place where heavenly rituals were offered.
2. The place where Gim Chunchu and Munhi (Gim Yusin's younger sister) were married.
3. A place where a portrait of Munno, the eighth leader of the Hwarang Knights, was enshrined.

By the way, the shape of the carved stone water canal in Poseokjeong emulated the Heavenly Garden constellation. How splendid a relic this has been throughout history!

In the past, water from Mt. Namsan would flow down past Poseokjeong, but no more water flows ever since a resevoir was established on the upper stream to serve nearby villages. In the old days, a large amount of water probably flowed vigorously enough to cover boulders. And Silla's royal family members must have performed their

음력 11월 추운 날 신라의 왕이 왕족들을 거느리고 그 좁은 데서 무슨 술
잔치를 벌이고 여흥을 즐겼겠어요? 그런데 그런 내용이 지금도 포석정 입
구 왼쪽 간판에 붙어 있습니다.

ablutions and auspicious ceremonies there. I am sure they prayed for their country's peace and prosperity.

Is it truly likely that the king of Silla, with the royal family members by his side, had a banquet with entertainments in that small space on a cold day in the eleventh lunar month? But that is what the information board says to the left of Poseokjeong entrance.

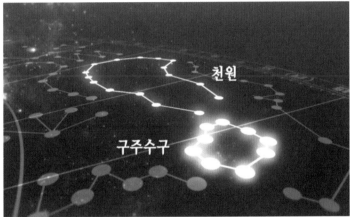

포석정의 형태는 천원天苑(하늘 정원) 별자리와 일치한다.
(출처: 다큐 〈첨성대 별기〉 중)
The shape of Poseokjeong accords with the Heavenly Garden constellation.
(Source: Documentary "Separate Notes on Cheomseongdae Observatory")

계욕장 | 길례와 천제를 올리기 전에 목욕재계를 하던 곳
A site for ablutions:
Here, people purified their bodies prior to performing auspicious ceremonies and heavenly rituals.

그리고 첨성대瞻星臺를 보면 우주 광명의 문화 역사 원형정신이 거기에 그대로 함축되어 있습니다. 첨성대 아랫부분을 보면 정사각형으로 돼 있습니다. 이것은 어머니 땅의 정신, 어머니 품을 근본으로 한 것입니다. 황도대라든지 태양이 지나가는 과정을 과학적으로 포물선을 그리면 건물이 이런 형상으로 나온다고 합니다. 그렇게 해서 전체는 361개 반의 돌을 세우고, 또 천상 28수 별자리를 본떠서 돌을 28단으로 했습니다. 또 둥근 것은 하늘 아버지의 마음, 생명, 신성을 나타냅니다.

첨성대의 곡선은
태양 궤도의 곡선과
일치한다.

동지
winter solstice

The curve of the body of
Cheomseongdae
Observatory matches the
curve of the solar orbit.

추분
autumn equinox

하지
summer solstice

In Cheomseongdae Observatory, the original spirit of the history and culture of cosmic radiance is reflected. The stylobate of the astronomical observatory is a square, which is based on mother earth's spirit or mother earth's arms (bosom); and it has a contour line that is said to have been built to reflect the ecliptic, which is the path that the sun follows. A total of 361.5 bricks were used in the body of the observatory, and the bricks were stacked into twenty-eight layers to emulate the Twenty-Eight Mansions. The round shape of the body implies father heaven's spirit, vitality, and divinity.

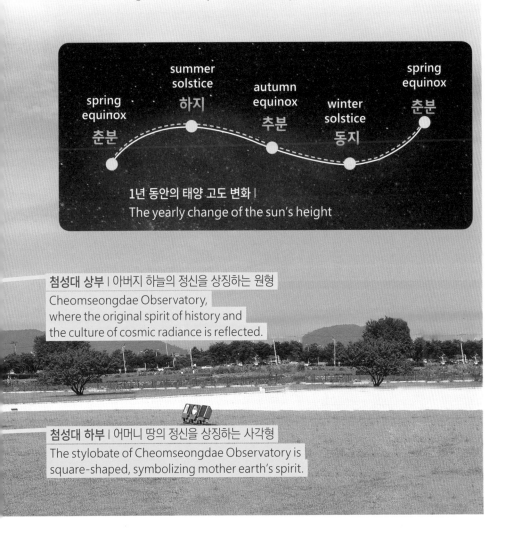

첨성대 상부 | 아버지 하늘의 정신을 상징하는 원형
Cheomseongdae Observatory, where the original spirit of history and the culture of cosmic radiance is reflected.

첨성대 하부 | 어머니 땅의 정신을 상징하는 사각형
The stylobate of Cheomseongdae Observatory is square-shaped, symbolizing mother earth's spirit.

그래서 천원지방天圓地方 사상, 천지부모 사상이 있습니다. 첨성대는 이 대우주 천지부모의 몸체를 상징하고 그 정신을 축약해 놓은 겁니다.

거기에다가 28수 황도대의 별자리를 축약하고, 1년 열두 달, 360일, 한 달 30일이라는 날수, 책력을 집어넣었습니다. 이런 천문, 시간과 공간의 근본정신을 여기에다 다 담아놓고 제일 위에 우물 정 자로 천정석天井石을 세웠습니다.

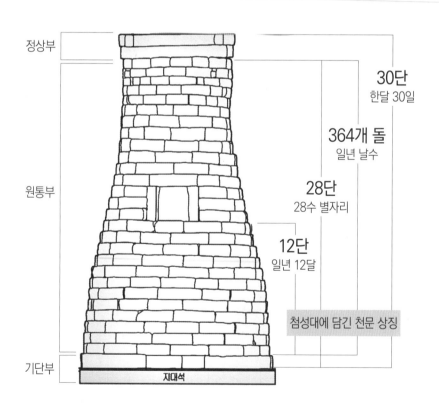

정상부

30단
한달 30일

364개 돌
일년 날수

28단
28수 별자리

원통부

12단
일년 12달

첨성대에 담긴 천문 상징

기단부

지대석

Thus, the concepts that heaven is round and earth is square, and that heaven is father and earth is mother, are reflected in the observatory; this symbolizes the bodies of father heaven and mother earth and their spirits.

In addition, the number "twenty-eight" in the "Twenty-Eight Mansions" was referenced. And the architectural design of the observatory also incorporated calendarial numbers: twelve, as in twelve months of a year; "364," the approximate numbers of the days within a year; and thirty, the number of the days in a month. At the peak of this combination of astronomical, temporal and spatial elements was placed a ceiling stone in the shape of the character *jeong* (井, "well").

우주광명의 문화·역사, 원형정신이 함축되어 있는 첨성대
대우주 천지부모의 몸체聖身를 축약한 첨성대

Cheomseongdae Observatory abridged the sacred bodies of the universe's father heaven and mother earth.
The body of Cheomseongdae Observatory is round-shaped, symbolizing father heaven's spirit.

Astronomical symbols contained in Cheomseongdae Observatory:

→ The body's 364 bricks symbolize the number of the days within a year.
→ The body's twenty-eight layers of bricks symbolize the Twenty-Eight Mansions.
→ The twelve layers of the lower body symbolize the twelve months in a year.
→ The thirty layers of the body's bricks symbolize the thirty days within a month.

우리말에 천정이라는 말이 있습니다. 천정이 낮다든지 천정이 높아서 멋있다든지 하는데, 천정이라는 게 무엇인가? 우리가 조선 왕조 궁궐을 가보면 임금님이 계신 곳은 지상의 천하를 다스리는 옥좌고, 그 위는 바로 우주, 하늘 천정입니다. 그런데 왜 그걸 하늘 천 자, 우물 정 자라고 하느냐? 그 정이 무엇인가? 예전에 시정잡배市井雜輩라는 말을 썼는데 그 시정이라는 것은 시장에 우물이 있다는 말인가? 나정, 알영정, 포석정 그리고 첨성대에 있는 천정석 우물 정 자의 그 신성함, 그 원형문화의 수수께끼는 무엇인가?

천문으로 보면 정井은 견우성*의 중심 별자리라 하는데, 천상열차분야지도天象列次分野之圖에 나오는 우주의 별자리, 그 별자리의 구조 질서를 그대로 신라 왕도에다가 투영시킨 것입니다. 그리고 그 중심에 첨성대가 있습니다.

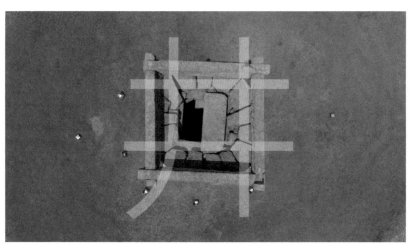

첨성대의 천정석天井石과 우물 정井 자를 겹친 모습
The ceiling stone of Cheomseongdae Observatory and the character *jeong*.

In the Korean language, there is a word *cheonjeong* [*cheon* means "heaven" and *jeong* means "well," but the combined meaning is "ceiling (s)"]. We say that the *cheonjeong* is low or that the *cheonjeong* is so high that it is stylish. What does the word *cheonjeong* signify? When we visit a palace from the Joseon Dynasty, we behold the king's throne from which the king governed the entire country; and the *cheonjeong* ("ceiling") above the throne implies the universe [but as mentioned before, the word *cheonjeong* also consists of *cheon* ("heaven") and *jeong* ("well")]. What is the significance of the term *jeong*? In the past, Koreans would use the expression *sijeong jabbae* [*si*, "marketplace"; *jeong*, "well"; *jab*, "vulgar"; *bae*, "fellows"]; and what is the connotation of *jeong* in *sijeong*, whose literal meaning is "marketplace well"? Moreover, what is the mystery of the divinity, or of the original culture, related to the character *jeong* widely found in place names such as Najeong, Alyeongjeong, Poseokjeong, and atop Cheomseongdae Observatory?

In terms of astronomy, *jeong* (井) is said to be the central constellation Cowherd.* The constellations of heaven marked on "The Chart of the Constellations and the Regions They Govern" were recreated exactly in that order in the Silla capital, and in the center of the layout was located Cheomseongdae Observatory.

Cowherd. There are differing opinions about to which star of Western astronomy "Cowherd" corresponds. Some believe it is Altair of the Eagles, while others assert it is Dabih of the Goat.

『환단고기』를 보면 환국과 배달의 역사에서, 우주광명의 환국의 문화 역사 정신을 가져온 환웅이 제일 먼저 한 것이 무엇인가? 안함로의 『삼성기』 상편을 보면 어떤 내용이 있습니까?

桓雄氏繼興하사 奉天神之詔하시고
환 웅 씨 계 흥   봉 천 신 지 조

鑿子井女井於天坪하시고
착 자 정 여 정 어 천 평

환웅씨가 환국을 계승하여 일어나 천신(상제님)의 가르침을 받들어
천평(백두산의 넓은 들판)에 자정子井과 여정女井을 파시고
(『환단고기』「삼성기」 上)

"후後에 환웅씨계흥桓雄氏繼興하사 봉천신지조奉天神之詔하시고", 환웅이 일어나서 천신의 가르침을 계승해서 "착자정여정어천평鑿子井女井於天坪", 천평, 하늘 평야에다가 자정과 여정을 팠다는 것입니다.

이것을 남자의 우물, 여자의 우물로 소탈하게 해석하기도 하지만, 실제

직녀 서양 천문학에서 거문고자리의 베가에 해당한다.

로는 자정과 여정이 마치 견우와 직녀*라든지, 28수의 별자리라든지, 아니면 우리가 지금 우물 정 자의 뜻을 파헤치려고 하는 바로 그 별과 관련이 있는 것입니다.

이 우물 정 자는 솟대를 네 개 세운 모습을 하고 있습니다. 이것 자체는 팔각, 여덟 개의 기둥 형상입니다. 나정을 보면 거기에 한 글귀가 있습니다. 입구 간판에 영문으로 같이 쓴 것을 보면, 여기에서 국가 의식을 행했다는 것입니다. 그래서 나정을 어떤 신궁으로 추정하고 있습니다.

According to *Hwandan Gogi*, what was it that Hwanung, who brought with him to Baedal Hwanguk's culture of cosmic radiance and the spirit of history, did first?

桓雄氏繼興하사 奉天神之詔하시고 鑿子井女井於天坪하시고

Hwanung established a nation that succeeded Hwanguk. He accepted the mandate of Sangjenim, the Heavenly God,

In Cheonpyeong (a spacious plain around Mt. Baekdusan), he excavated two kinds of wells, known as *jajeong* and *yeo-jeong*....

(Source: "Samseong Gi I" *Hwandan Gogi*)

What does *Samseong Gi I* say in relation to this question? It says, "Later, Hwanung established a nation that succeeded Hwanguk. He accepted the mandate of Sangjenim, the Heavenly God.... In Cheonpyeong, he excavated two kinds of wells, known as *jajeong* and *yeojeong*...."

The names *jajeong* and *yeojeong* may be simply interpreted as wells for men and women respectively. Yet, in fact, these wells are related to Cowherd and Weaver Girl,* the Twenty-Eight Mansions, and to the star that we are now to discuss as we delve into the meaning of the character *jeong*.

Weaver Girl. Corresponds to the star Vega in Western astronomy.

The character *jeong* (井, "well") has the shape of four erected sacred poles. The shape made by linking the end of each pole of the character is octagonal. There is a phrase related to Najeong. According to what is written in English on the information board at the entrance, national ceremonies were held there. Such being the case, Najeong is presumed to have been a shrine for a progenitor or something similar.

이 정이라는 문양은 전 세계적으로 나옵니다. 수메르 문명권에서도 이 우물을 '우문umun'이라 해서 발음이 비슷합니다. 그런데 첨성대 천정석처럼 저렇게 우물 정 자로 되어 있습니다. 저것은 무슨 별이나 무엇을 상징하는 것입니다. 우리가 그 당시 원형문자를 해석해야 되는데요.

홍산紅山 옥기 가운데 태양신을 상징하는 것을 보면 거기에 우물 정 자 무늬가 있습니다. 태양신의 머리 쪽에 왜 우물 정 자가 있는가? 이것도 우리가 한번 곰곰이 생각해 볼 문제입니다.

수메르 문명의 '정井' 자 문양 | 우문(umun) = 우물
(조철수, 「수메르어·국어고어 문법범주 대조분석」, 『언어학』 19호)

The *jeong* character (井) pattern of Sumerian civilization
/umun/ = /umul/
(Source: "Comparison and Analysis of the Grammar
Categories between Sumerian and Ancient Korean
Language" by Jo Cheol-su, *Linguistics*, journal series no. 19.)

This *jeong* character (井) pattern is seen worldwide. In the Sumerian civilization, the word for 'well' was "*umun*," which is similar to "*umul*," the Korean word for 'well.' In addition to the similarity of the word, Sumerian wells also resembled the shape of *jeong* (井) just like the ceiling stone of Cheomseongdae Observatory. That pattern probably symbolizes a certain star or something similar. Now, we need to interpret the letters from that time.

In terms of jade artifacts from the Hongshan culture, some that symbolize the sun god have the *jeong* character (井) pattern. Why is there the *jeong* character pattern on the sun god's head? It is another issue we should ponder.

홍산문화 옥기 속 '정井' 자 문양 I 태양신 머리에 왜 우물 정井 자가 있는가?
The *jeong* character (井) pattern is seen on jade artifacts of Hongshan culture.
Why is there the *jeong* character (井) pattern on the sun god's head?

그리고 이 솟터의 우물 정 자 문화는 무엇인가? 개성開城에도 천문대가 있고, 조선왕조 기록을 보면 바로 평양 남쪽에 똑같은 이름의 첨성대가 있었습니다. 개성의 천문대도 우물 정 자 식으로 해서 네 개 기둥을 박아놨습니다.

城內…有瞻星臺。

(평양)성 안에 첨성대가 있다. (『조선왕조실록』「세종실록지리지」)

이 우물 정 자 문화의 원형은 바로 원십자原十字, 우주의 원십자 문화입니다. 이 우주의 원십자 문화에서 절을 상징하는 만卍 자가 나왔습니다.

井	우물 정
✚	우물 정자의 원형, 원십자
卍	만자 민

고려시대 첨성대 | 황해도 개성
Cheomseongdae Observatory during the Goryeo Dynasty
Gaeseong, Hwanghae-do Province

What does the existence of the character *jeong* (井) pattern at the sites of the sacred poles suggest? In Gaeseong [the capital of the Goryeo Dynasty], there was also an astronomical observatory (during the Goryeo Dynasty). Additionally, according to a record of the Joseon Dynasty, there was a Cheomseongdae Observatory in the south of Pyeongyang that shares the name with that in Gyeongju. The astronomical observatory in Gaeseong also had four pillars driven into the ground in the shape of the *jeong* character (井) pattern.

城內···有瞻星臺。
"Inside the city [Pyeongyang], there is Cheomseongdae."
(Source: "Geography Section of the Annals of King Sejong"
in *Annals of the Joseon Dynasty*)

The origin of this *jeong* character was the primal form of the cross—that is, the primal cross of the universe. From this primal cross originated the Buddhist *man* character (卍), symbolizing Buddhist temples.

Jeong (井, "Well")
The origin of the *jeong* character is the primal cross. (✚)
The *man* character: (卍)

The *man* character (卍) patterns are seen on pillars of the Hagia Sophia in Turkey, the center of the Byzantine cultural spirit and religion located in the former land of the Ottoman Empire. How did it happen that a symbol of Buddhist temples—the *man* character (卍) patterns—was arranged on the pillars of the cathedral? Was it because something had gone wrong with the brain of the architect who built the cathedral about fifteen hundred years ago?

이런 만 자 문양이 오스만 제국의 동로마 그 비잔틴 문화 정신, 종교문화의 본부라 할 수 있는 지금의 튀르키예 소피아 성당 기둥에 있습니다. 1,500년 전에 성당의 건축가가 머리가 잘못되어서 절을 상징하는 만 자를 쭉 나열했을까요?

　　이것은 바로 '천지와 인간은 한마음이다, 하늘과 땅과 인간의 마음은 사방으로 이렇게 반듯하다'는 사정방四正方의 마음, 우주 시공간의 본성인 사정방의 바른 마음, 도심, 우주 도의 마음, 생명의 마음, 영원불변의 진리의 마음, 신성한 그 마음을 상징하는 것입니다. 이런 원십자 문화가 수만 년 전부터, 그리고 만 자 문양이 석가 탄생 이전 수수 천 년 전부터 내려옵니다.

비잔틴 건축의 걸작 하기아 소피아 대성당 |
튀르키예 이스탄불, 537년 건축

The pattern symbolizes the mind of the four cardinal directions, signifying that heaven, earth, and humanity are of one mind and that the mind of heaven, earth, and humanity is upright in four cardinal directions—that is, it signifies the righteous mind of four cardinal directions (which is the nature of time and space in the universe), the mind of dao, the mind of the dao of the universe, the mind of life, the mind of eternal truth, and the divine mind. This primal cross culture and the *man* character (卍) patterns were passed down from tens of thousands of years ago and from thousands of years before Shakyamuni's birth respectively.

A masterpiece of Byzantine architecture, the Hagia Sophia was constructed in 537. Istanbul, Turkey

성당 내부의 만卍 자 문양ㅣ
The *man* character (卍) patterns inside the cathedral

제가 러시아 역사가 처음 시작된 우크라이나의 박물관을 가보니까 그 전시장 끝 오른쪽 아래에 저 원십자, 우물 정 자가 밥그릇에 저렇게 뚜렷하게 새겨져 있었습니다. 여러 가지 우물 정 자 문양이 여기저기 박물관에 있습니다.

그런데 신라에서 나온, 광개토왕의 명호를 써놓은, 호우라는 병 그릇의 끝에 보면 열 십 자가 있습니다. 그리고 제일 위에 우물 정 자 문양이 있습니다.

일찍이 소설가 최인호가 이 수수께끼를 풀고 싶어서 『왕도의 비밀』이라는 소설을 내면서, 이 우물 정 자를 추적하기 위해서 우리나라 저 북쪽과 중국으로 해서, 백두산 천지까지 오른 적이 있습니다. 그래서 이것은 백두산 천지의 생명수도 상징한다고 말했습니다.

신라의 첨성대에 우주의 3원 28수 별을 집어넣었는데, 그 별들을 관장하는 우주 역사의 중심지는 과연 어디인가? 인간과 신의 사회를 다스리는 신정한 우주 역사의 심장부가 어디냐? 왕들은 그것을 알고 있었습니다. 그것을 각성과 이해가 아니라 신교의 일방적 깨달음의 신성한 의식 속에서 천상의 조상들로부터 그 별들로부터 국가 안위에 대해서 또는 어떤 경책의 메시지로서 늘 들었기 때문입니다.

천문대 수장 정도 되면 왜 첨성대 위에다가 천정석을 놓았는지 그 비밀이 무엇인지 알았을 것입니다. 인간이 몸을 받아가지고 태어나는 우주 역사의 가장 신성한 중심별, 바로 그것이 북녘 하늘의 별인데 그게 무엇인가?

Russian history first started in Ukraine, and when I was in the History Museum of Ukraine, I saw on the right side at the end of the exhibition hall a bowl with the primal cross, or the *jeong* character (井) pattern, clearly engraved on its surface. Different patterns of *jeong* characters (井) are seen here and there in that museum.

By the way, on the bottom of a bowl excavated from Silla soil is engraved the posthumus title of Goguryeo King Gwanggaeto, and on the edge of the engravings is seen a cross pattern. At the top of the engravings is a *jeong* character (井) pattern.

Korean novelist Choe In-ho attemped to solve this riddle in his novel *The Secret of the Royal Capital*. As part of the preparatory work for his novel, he traveled the northern regions of Korea and China, and even went to Lake Cheonji on top of Mt. Baekdusan, in his pursuit of the character *jeong*. Consequently, he asserted that the *jeong* character symbolizes the life water of Lake Cheonji on Mt. Baekdusan.

The Silla people incorporated the Three Enclosures and Twenty-Eight Mansions of the universe into Cheomseongdae Observatory. Then what is the center of cosmic history that governs those stars? What is the true heart of cosmic history that governs both humans and the spirits? Kings in ancient times knew these answers not by comprehension and awakening, but by diligently listening—during a state of divine consciousness brought about by enlightenment from Spirit Teaching—to their ancestors in heaven and to stars speaking to them concerning the wellbeing of their country or issuing messages of admonition.

The leader of the astronomical observatory must have known a secret concerning the ceiling stone when the ceiling stone was placed on top of Cheomseongdae Observatory. The most sacred central constellation of cosmic history, from which humans are born, is located in the northern sky. What is it?

우크라이나 키예프 역사박물관 I
Kyiv History Museum, Ukraine

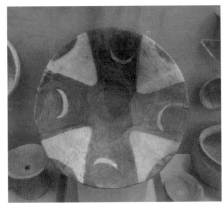

원십자 무늬 그릇 | 6천 년 전
A bowl with primal cross patterns
from 6,000 years ago

우물 정 자 무늬 그릇 | 6천 년 전
A bowl with the *jeong* character
pattern from 6,000 years ago

청동 호우壺杅 | 5세기. 경주 호우총 출토. 국립경주박물관
A bronze bowl from the fifth century, excavated from Tomb of the Bowl in
Gyeongju
Gyeongju National Museum

바로 상투의 본래 말인 상두上斗, 천상의 두성斗星입니다. 9천 년 역사에서 소도 제천문화에서, 온 인류가 섬겨온 천제문화의 주인공인 바로 우주 역사 통치자 삼신상제님이 계시는 천상 옥좌의 별이 바로 북두칠성입니다.

그 칠성의 별을 보면, 대괴 탐랑, 거문, 녹존, 문곡, 그 다음에 염정, 무곡, 파군 이렇게 있습니다. 그래서 칠성인데, 원 상제님이 계신 별하고 그 아들이 되는 천자의 별을 좌보우필左輔右弼이라 해서 두 개가 더 있습니다. 그래서 북두구진北斗九辰이라 합니다.

첫째 탐랑과 거문, 녹존, 문곡 머리에 있는 이 네 개 별을 선기璇璣라 하고, 그 뒤 세 별을 옥형玉衡이라 합니다. 일본의 역사라는 것은 이걸 그대로 따간 것입니다. 삼신과, 칠성으로 해서 일곱 신이 이 우주 역사와 인간의 창세 역사를 열었다고 합니다. 그래 뒤에 네 개 별의 신들을 부부로 배치해서, 이자나기(伊耶那岐), 이자나미(伊耶那美)가 나와서 일본의 여덟 개 섬을 만들었다, 창세 역사를 열었다는 이야기를 하는 것입니다.

기독교의 아버지와 아들 성령문화의 총 결론도 일곱 성령입니다. 그래 요한이 천상에 올라가서 백보좌의 아버지 하나님을 직접 뵈었는데 그 아버지 하나님의 앞에 일곱 등불이 있었습니다. 일곱 개의 별을 본 것처럼 그대로 계시록에 기록해 놨습니다.

The answer is *sangdu*, the original Korean term for "topknot," and it also indicates the 'Highest Stars' (aka, the 'Seven Stars') in heaven. Throughout Korea's some nine-thousand-year history, in the culture of offering heavenly rituals at *sodo*s, humanity worshipped Samsin Sangjenim, the Ruler of the Universe, who was the focus of heavenly rituals. And the constellation of the heavenly throne where Samsin Sangjenim resides is the Seven Stars of the northern sky.

The Seven Stars in the northern sky consist of Tamrang, Geomun, Nokjon, Mungok, Yeomjeong, Mugok, and Pagun. Actually, there are two more stars located near them: one for Sangjenim and one for his son, that is, the Son of Heaven. These two stars are assistants from the left and right. Thus, altogether these are named the 'Nine Stars of the Northern Dipper.'

The four stars in the bowl section of the Big Dipper—Tamrang, Geomun, Nokjon, and Mungok—are called the 'Seongi.' The other three stars are the 'Okhyeong.' Japanese history emulates such star systems: in addition to three deities, the seven deities of the Big Dipper started the history of the universe and brought about humanity's creation. Later, the deities of four stars were bound together as husband and wife; and the couple formed from this union, Izanagi and Izanami, emerged to create the eight islands of Japan, and that is the story of how the world's history started.

The core idea of Christianity's Father, Son, and the Holy Spirit is the Seven Spirits of God. When John ascended to heaven and in person met God the Father on the white throne, there were seven lamps before God the Father. It is described in the Book of Revelation that he witnessed seven stars.

하나님의 일곱 영이 성령인데 이 성령문화도 잘못되어 그냥 아버지 영, 아들 영으로만 이야기합니다. 올바른 성령문화가 아직 안 나온 것입니다. 기독교 2천 년 역사에서도 성령은 일곱 영인데, 일곱 영이 무엇인지 구체적으로 모르는 것입니다. 알 수가 없잖아요, 말씀을 안 하셨으니까.

사도 요한의 아버지 하느님의 성령 친견 | 「요한 계시록」 1장, 4장
John the Evangelist's witnessing of the Holy Spirit
(Source: The Book of Revelation 1 and 4)

As a matter of fact, the seven spirits of God are the Holy Spirit, but they were erroneously termed only the Father's spirit and the Son's spirit. A correct understanding of the Holy Spirit has not yet been established. Throughout the two-thousand-year-long history of Christianity, the Holy Spirit has been seven spirits, but it has not been known what the seven spirits specifically indicate. People have had no idea because God did not specify this.

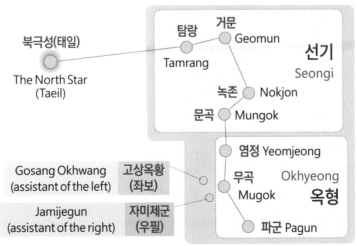

북두구진

The Nine Stars of the Northern Dipper

그런데 이것이 천문으로 볼 때는 바로 치우 천황의 스승이신 자부 선사紫府仙師가 처음 칠성력 책력을 만들었고 여기서 동아시아의 책력 문화가 구체화되었습니다.

이 우물 정 자 문화라는 것은 바로 천지와 일월과 모든 별을 다스리는 이 생명의 중심이 되는 별, 우주 역사 통치자 삼신상제님이 머무시는 옥좌가 있는 별과 연관이 있습니다. 솟터의 **우물 정 자 비밀은 인간과 신의 세계를 다스리는 우주 통치자의 천상 궁전이 있는 칠성을 상징하는 것입니다.**

그래서 우리 조상들은 옛날부터 상투를 틀었고, 홍산문화에서도 5,500년 전 제사장의 무덤을 보면 상투를 틀고 꽂았던 옥고玉箍가 있습니다. 상투는 소도 신앙의 상징인데, 이 상투 문화가 바로 우물 정 자의 문화 정신을 그대로 대변하고 있는 것입니다.

상투를 고정하는 옥고玉箍
A jade frame for fixing a topknot

5,500년 전 제사장(왕) |
우하량 제2지점 1호묘
A chief priest (or a king) from 5,500 years ago
The first tomb of the second excavation site, Niuheliang Village

In terms of astronomy, an immortal master, Jabu, the teacher of Heavenly Emperor Chiu, made the Chilseongryeok Calendar ("Seven Star Calendar") for the first time, and from that time began the use of calendars in East Asia.

The use of the character *jeong* ("well") is related to the central star of life that governs heaven and earth, the sun and moon, and all the other stars. It is also related to the star that is the location of the throne of Samsin Sangjenim, the ruler of cosmic history. The secret of the character *jeong* ("well") is that it symbolizes the Seven Stars, the location of the heavenly palace of the cosmic ruler, who governs the worlds of both humanity and the spirits.

By the way, the ancestors of Koreans tied their hair in a topknot from ancient times, and in a tomb of a chief priest (or a king) of the Hongshan culture from 5,500 years ago, a jade frame for fixing a topknot was excavated. The topknot is a symbol of the custom of *sodo*s, and the practice of tying a topknot indicates the cultural spirit of the character *jeong* ("well").

신라 문화의 중심 코드

신라 문화의 중심 코드는 인류의 창세 원형문화의 칠성문화, 태일문화, 삼신문화입니다. 바로 그것이 오늘 북 콘서트의 아주 자랑스러운 궁극의 메시지입니다.

① 칠성七星 문화

신라 6촌장의 비밀은 단군조선의 12소도의 압축판으로서, 우주 창세 경전 「천부경」의 '대삼합육大三合六', 하늘과 땅, 인간이 하나가 되면 거기서 6이라는 우주의 영원한 생명수가 열린다는 것입니다. 여기에서 실제 우주의 역사를 구성하고 다스리는 칠성이라든지 영원한 불멸의 생명 8이라든지 또 그 왕도를 상징하는 아홉 수 즉 7, 8, 9의 문화정신이 생성된 것입니다.

천부경의 '대삼합육大三合六'

대삼大三	하늘·땅·인간이
합合	하나가 되면
육六	영원한 생명수 '육(6)'이 열린다

6촌장이 중심에 박혁거세 왕을 모시는 것이 바로 칠성문화입니다. 또 신라에는 왕이 되는 아홉 개의 성씨가 있습니다. 박·석·김 성씨 세 개와 6촌장의 여섯 성씨를 합하면 아홉 성씨입니다. 이것은 북두구진의 바로 그 9수를 상징합니다. 신라는 진한을 이었으므로, 환국·배달·조선을 계승한, 그 왕도문화의 정신을 계승한 중심 지배세력입니다. 이것도 북두문화의 정신을 벗어나지 않는다고 봅니다.

The Central Codes of the Silla Culture

The central codes of the Silla culture were the Seven Stars culture, the culture of Taeil, and the culture of Samsin, which were all from the primordial culture in the era of humanity's creation. That is the very proud ultimate message of today's lecture.

① Seven Stars Culture

The secret of Silla's six village heads is that they were an abridgement of the twelve *sodo*s of Dangun Joseon, and that, as suggested in *Chenbu Gyeong* (*"Scripture of Heavenly Code"*), when heaven, earth, and humanity are united, this gives rise to Six, the cosmic number of eternal life. And then Six gives rise to the cultural concepts of the numbers Seven (the Seven Stars that actually form and govern cosmic history), Eight (immortal life), and Nine (which symbolizes royal statesmanship).

"The Great Three unite into Six …"
(From the *Chenbu Gyeong* (*"Scripture of Heavenly Code"*))

The Great Three unite into Six	When heaven, earth, and humanity unite, they give rise to Six, the number of eternal life.

The custom that the six villages' heads placed their king, Bak Hyeokgeose, at their center and served him reflects the Seven Stars culture. Besides, in Silla, there were nine clans qualified to have members ascend to royalty: the three royal clans of Bak, Seok, and Gim, plus the clans of the six villages. These nine clans symbolized the number nine of the Northern Dipper's nine stars. Having succeeded Jinhan, Silla was the central ruling power that was the successor to Hwanguk, Baedal, and Joseon, and the inheritor of the spirit of their royal statesmanship. Such a succession also seems to accord with the spirit of the Northern Dipper culture.

신라 역사에 흐르는 천부경의 정신

❖❖❖

박혁거세왕(1) + 육촌장(6)   칠성문화(7)

영원한 불멸의 생명   팔(8)

박석김(3) + 육촌장(6)   북두구진(9)

   신라 진흥왕眞興王 12년(551년)에 팔관회八觀會가 나왔습니다. 이 팔관회라는 것은 본래 불교 행사가 아닙니다. 영원불멸의 생명, 신선을 상징하는 8을 근본으로 해서 가을의 추수감사제를 천신, 지신, 수신에게 올린 것입니다.

   이 소도의 천제문화가 팔관회로 계승됐고, 이것이 고려시대에도 지속되었습니다. 그리고 팔관회가 일본에 넘어가서 하치만(八幡) 신앙으로 정착되어 있습니다.

소도 제천문화의 전승 과정

❖❖❖

단군조선 소도문화 ▶ 신라 팔관회 ▶ 고려 팔관회

                  ↳ 일본 팔번八幡(하치만) 신앙

The Spirit of the *Cheonbu Gyeong* (*"Scripture of Heavenly Code"*) Flowing Through the History of Silla

King Bak Hyeokgeose (1) + Six Villages' Heads (6)	The Seven Stars Culture (7)
Immortal Life	Eight (8)
Bak, Seok, Gim (3) + Six Villages' Heads (6)	Nine Stars of the Northern Dipper (9)

In the twelfth year of King Jinheung's reign (551), Palgwanhoe ("Festival of Eight Vows") was introduced. Contrary to popular belief, Palgwanhoe was not a Buddhist event at first. It was a harvest festival offering to Heavenly God and to the spirits of the earth and of water, based upon the number eight, which symbolizes immortal life.

The tradition of offering heavenly rituals at *sodo*s was transformed into Palgwanhoe ("Festival of Eight Vows"), and Palgwanhoe continued throughout the Goryeo Dynasty. When Palgwanhoe was transmitted to Japan, it took root as the faith in the Hachiman Spirit.

The Transmission Process of Heavenly Rituals Held at Sodos

Dangun Joseon : The Tradition of Sodos

▶ Silla: Palgwanhoe ⇸ Japan: Faith in the Hachiman Spirit
▶ Goryeo: Palgwanhoe

하치만 신사는 구주九州 북쪽과 경도京都, 그리고 동경東京 에도막부에 하나씩 있습니다. 하치만 신사의 중심은 구주에 있는 것이라 하는데, 구주 북쪽을 가보면 이 신사에서는 절을 네 번 합니다. 이 우주의 '생칠팔구生 七八九', 칠성문화에서 영원한 우주의 불멸의 생명 신선의 도를 열어주시는 데 바로 그 주인 되시는, 모든 신선과 모든 부처, 동서 신인들의 근원이 되는 우주의 삼신상제님, 우주의 진정한 아버지 하나님을 배례하기 때문입니다. 그래서 일본의 구주 우사하치만(宇佐八幡) 신궁에서는 네 번 절을 합니다.

제가 도쿄에 있는 하치만 신궁을 가서 감동하고 참 부러웠던 것이 있습니다. 일본 사람들이 신사를 아주 소중히 여긴다는 것입니다. 가마쿠라 막부의 쓰루오카(鶴岡)를 이번에 방문했는데 박물관에 가보면 그 시내의 전체 지도가 있습니다.

The Three Major Hachiman Shrines in Japan

일본의 3대
하치만八幡 신사

이와시미즈하치만궁
Iwashimizu Hachiman Shrine

우사하치만궁
Usa Hachiman Shrine

가마쿠라
Kamakura

교토
Kyoto

큐슈
Kyushu

쓰루오카하치만궁
Tsurugaoka Hachiman Shrine

The Hachiman shrines are located in the north of Kyushu, Kyoto, and the district in Tokyo where the former Edo feudal government was located. The principal such shrine was the one in Kyushu, and visitors bow four times in this shrine. The object of their worship is the universe's Samsin Sangjenim—the very God the Father of the universe—who grants the dao of the immortals or the universe's eternal life, and he who is also the foundation of all immortals, buddhas, and divine persons of the East and the West. Given the object of their worship, visitors of the Hachiman Shrine in Kyushu bow four times.

There is one thing that impressed me and made me jealous when I visited the Hachiman Shrine located in Tokyo: the Japanese really value their shrines. I also visited Tsurugaoka, the location of the former Kamakura feudal government, and saw a map of the entire city in the museum there.

우사하치만신궁宇佐八幡神宮 | Usa Hachiman Shrine
큐슈 오이타현   Oita Prefecture, Kyushu

우백호
White Tiger on the right

좌청룡
Green Dragon on the left

쓰루오카하치만궁 주변의 지리地理
Geomancy surrounding the Tsurugaoka Hachiman Shrine

그 중심 도로가 시가지 가운데에 한 일 자로 쫙 이렇게 닦여 있는데 그 위에 좌청룡, 우백호 산세가 뻗어 내려오고 아래는 바다가 넘실거립니다. 그 위쪽 끝점에 바로 하치만 신궁이 있습니다.

쿄토 하치만 신사에는 이 3수를 상징하는 삼태극이 기왓장 아래에 꽉 차 있습니다. 그것은 삼신문화 사상을 나타냅니다.

일본의 하치만 신앙은 신라의 화랑도가 가서 전한 것이고, 여기에 삼신과 칠성이라든지 미륵신앙, 태양신 신앙이 융합되어서 영원불멸을 상징하는 팔번, 8수, 팔관의 정신이 계승되고 있습니다.

쓰루오카하치만궁
鶴岡八幡宮
The Hachiman Shrine
located in
Tsurugaoka

The main road stretched straight through the middle of the city. The geomantic features of the mountain involved the Green Dragon on the left and the White Tiger on the right; and there is a rolling sea beneath the mountain. The Hachiman shrine is located at the end of the upper side.

In the Hachiman Shrine of Kyoto, many tricolored Taegeuk patterns symbolizing the number three are painted below the roofing tiles. The patterns represent Samsin culture. The origin of Japan's Hachiman faith was transmitted by the Hwarang Knights from Silla and then combined with the concepts of Samsin, the Seven Stars, and the faith in Maitreya and in a sun god; thus, the spirit of the "eight vows" of Palgwanhoe, or the spirit of valuing the number eight, which symbol-

izes immortality, endures in the form of the faith in Hachiman (*hachi* means the number "eight").

삼수문화의 상징 삼태극 |
The tricolored Taegeuk: the symbol of the tradition of valuing the number "three"

①-1. 화랑문화

신라 화랑문화의 뿌리는 배달의 삼랑, 단군조의 국자랑입니다. 화랑은 삼신을 수호하는 제사장 문화인데 『화랑세기花郞世紀』 서문에, "화랑자선도야花郞者仙徒也… 고자선도지이봉신위주古者仙徒只以奉神爲主"라 해서 화랑은 신선도를 닦는 사람인데, 옛날에 선도는 단지 신을 받드는 일을 위주로 하였다고 했습니다.

화 랑 자 선 도 야　　　고 자　선 도 지 이 봉 신 위 주
花郞者, 仙徒也。 … 古者, 仙徒只以奉神爲主。

화랑은 신선도를 닦는 사람이다. … 옛날에 선도는 단지 신(天神)을 받드는 일을 위주로 하였다. (『화랑세기』 서문)

이 선도는 유·불·선의 선이 아닙니다. 영원불멸의 우주광명 문화를 체득한 환국·배달·조선에서 내려오는 신교의 원형, 그 도통문화 정신을 말하는 것입니다. 이 사람들은 옛날에 지이봉신위주只以奉神爲主, 단지 신을 받드는 것을 위주로 했습니다. 신을 받드는, 신을 위해 사는, 신과 하나가 되는, 신의 신성과 생명과 그 힘과 창조력을 직접 역사에 발휘하는 것은 얼마나 과감하고 강력한가요? 이것이 바로 신라 역사문화를 움직인 힘, 위대한 삼국 통일의 저력이 되었던 것입니다.

①-1. Silla's Hwarang Knights Culture

The roots of Silla's Hwarang Knights culture were the Samnang of Baedal and the Gukjarang of Dangun Joseon. The Hwarang Knights institution was a sort of chief priest system that guarded Samsin. According to the Preface to *Hwarang Segi*, "The Hwarang Knights are people who cultivate the dao of immortality, ⋯ in ancient times, the main task of cultivating the dao of immortality was only worshipping God."

花郞者, 仙徒也。⋯ 古者, 仙徒只以奉神爲主。

The Hwarang Knights are people who cultivate the dao of immortality....

In ancient times, the main task of cultivating the dao of immortality was only worshipping God.

(Source: Preface to *Hwarang Segi*)

"Dao of immortality" in this context does not refer to the Immortalism that is listed together with such major eastern religions as Confucianism and Buddhism. It indicates the original Spirit Teaching or its cultural spirit of enlightenment that was passed down from the eras of Hwanguk, Baedal, and Joseon, the time when people learned by experience the culture of eternal cosmic radiance. These people who practiced the dao of immortality in ancient times only focused on worshipping God. How determined and powerful are the acts of worshipping God, living for God, becoming one with God, and displaying God's divinity, vitality, strength, and the creative power of God in history! Such acts became the very driving force advancing Silla's history and culture, providing the energy potential to achieve the grand unification of the Three Kingdoms.

신라 문화의 내면에는 칠성문화가 있습니다. 그래서 김유신金庾信 장군이 그 사조직으로 일곱 사람을 사귀었습니다.

유신공이 알천공, 임종공, 술종공 등 일곱 벗으로 칠성회를 만들어서, 칠성문화의 도를 사모하고 그것을 계승한 칠성우七星友와 남산에서 놀았다는 이야기가 『화랑세기』에도 나옵니다.

國有大事, 庾信公
(국유대사 유신공)

開七星會, 必問於公。
(개칠성회 필문어공)

나라에 큰 일이 있으면 유신공이 칠성회를 열어 반드시 공에게 물었다.

(『화랑세기』 16세 보종공)

七星友會遊南山。
(칠성우회유남산)

(신교 칠성문화의 도를 계승한) 일곱 화랑(칠성랑)이 모여 남산에서 놀았다.

(『화랑세기』 14세 호림공)

이 화랑의 문화는 군인 문화가 아닙니다. 화랑들은 환국·배달 이후의 낭가사상, 즉 우주광명 인간의 도의 정신을 가지고 있었습니다. 자기 스스로 신교 소도문화 성지에서 오상지도五常之道 심법을 전수 받아서 국가를 위해서 아주 과감하게 싸우고 친구를 위해서 의리를 지켰습니다.

우리가 잘 알고 있는 사다함斯多含이 15세를 갓 넘었을 때 신라가 대가야를 멸망시켰습니다. 사다함은 자기 친구 무관랑武官郎이 병들어 죽었을 때 그 의리 때문에 애통해 하다가 7일 만에 그냥 죽어버렸습니다. 화랑 관창官昌이라든지, 박제상朴堤上, 김유신 장군의 담대함, 지혜도 엿볼 수 있습니다.

The Seven Stars culture was inherent in Silla culture. For example, Silla's General Gim Yusin had a private social club of seven people. There is a narrative in *Hwarang Segi* asserting that Gim Yusin formed the Club of Seven Stars, which included nobles such as Alcheon, Imjong, Suljong, and he associated at Mt. Namsan with the club members, who worshipped and inherited the cultural tradition of the Seven Stars.

國有大事, 庾信公 開七星會, 必問於公。

Regarding issues of important national affairs, Lord Gim Yusin surely held a meeting of the Club of Seven Stars and asked their opinions.
(Source: "Lord Bojong: Sixteenth Leader of the Hwarang Knights" *Hwarang Segi*)

七星友會遊南山。

Friends belonging to the Club of Seven Stars (who inherited Spirit Teaching's Seven Stars culture) gathered and socialized at Mt. Namsan.
(Source: "Lord Horim: Fourteenth Leader of the Hwarang Knights" *Hwarang Segi*)

The culture associated with the Hwarang Knights was not a military culture. Members of the Hwarang Knights possessed the Nang's philosophy, which originated from the era of Hwanguk and Baedal—that is, the dao spirit of the humanity of cosmic radiance. They personally accepted the mindset of the Five Constant Ways in Spirit Teaching's sacred *sodo* sites, fought bravely for the country, and remained loyal to their friends.

When a renowned leader of the Hwarang Knights, Sadaham, had just reached the age of fifteen, Silla destroyed the kingdom of Dae Gaya. Sadaham, a war hero, grieved bitterly when his friend Mugwanrang died of illness; and in a passion of grief, he followed his friend to

세속오계

충忠	사군이충事君以忠	박제상, 관창, 김영윤
효孝	사친이효事親以孝	효종랑, 향덕
신信	교우이신交友以信	김유신, 검군
용勇	임전무퇴臨戰無退	원술랑, 귀산과 추항
인仁	살생유택殺生有擇	사다함

　구주의 히코산에 가보면 환국 배달 조선의 주신 환인, 환웅, 단군을 모신 삼신궁이 있습니다.

　히코산 신궁神宮에는 후지와라강유(藤原桓雄)의 환웅화桓雄畵가 있고, 윷놀이판도 보존되어 있습니다. 이것은 화랑도가 건너와 산속의 동굴에서 3.7일 수행을 하며, 수험도로 정착한 것입니다. 히코산英彦山은 원래 히코산日子山으로 태양의 아들이 머문다는 뜻입니다.

후지야마 환웅藤山桓雄 | 히코산신궁 수험도관
Hwanung Fujiyama
Shugendo Training Center, Hikosan
Jingu Shrine

도복을 차려 입은 환웅桓雄 | 히코산신궁의 환웅숭배
Hwanung in practice suit
Worship of Hwanung, Hikosan Jingu
Shrine

the grave just seven days later. We can also additionally glimpse courage and wisdom in the cases of: a leader of the Hwarang Knights, Gwanchang; a loyal retainer, Bak Je-sang; and General Gim Yusin.

The Five Commandments for Laymen and Exemplary Figures

Loyalty	Serve the king with loyalty.	Bak Jesang, Gwanchang, Gim Yeongyun
Filial piety	Serve one's parents with filial piety.	Hyojong, Hyangdeok
Faith	Make friends with faith.	Gim Yusin, Geomgun
Bravey	Never retreat on the battlefield.	Wonsul, Gwisan and Chuhang
Benevolence	Be discriminating about the taking of life.	Sadaham

In Mt. Hikosan of Kyushu, there is a palace dedicated to three divine beings, where Hwanin, Hwanung, and Dangun—of Hwanguk, Baedal, and Joseon—are enshrined. In Hikosan Jingu Shrine, there is a portrait of Hwanung Fujiwara, and the Yut-nori board is also preserved. When the teachings of the Hwarang Knights were transmitted from Silla to Japan, people underwent ascetic practices for three seven-day periods (that is, twenty-one days) in a mountain cave, and this practice later took root as Shugendo ("Way of Trial and Practice") in Hikosan Jingu Shrine. The characters for Mt. Hikosan were originally 日子山, which signify 'a mountain where the son of the sun resides.'

히코산신궁 I
Hikosan Jingu Shrine

상궁
Upper shrine

중궁
Middle shrine

하궁
Lower shrine

수험도관修驗道館 I 히코산신궁
Shugendo Training Center,
Hikosan Jingu Shrine

수험도관 I 환웅 동상
Shugendo Training Center:
A statue of Hwanung

상궁上宮 | 환국·환인
Upper shrine | Hwanguk: Hwanin

해발1,200m
1,200 meters above sea level

중궁中宮 | 배달·환웅
Middle shrine | Baedal: Hwanung

다마야玉屋신사
Tamaya Shrine

히코英彦산 신궁 배치도 | 규슈 후쿠오카현
Locations of Hikosan Jingu Shrine, Fukuoka Prefecture, Kyushu

고구려 멸망 후에는 조의선인이 사무라이와 수험도 문화를 정착시킵니다. 고구려 유민들이 관동지방과 동경 근처를 개척하는데, 유민들은 말을 기르고 무예를 연마하여 사무라이 문화의 토대를 놓았습니다. 오이소大磯 지역에는 고마高麗 신사가 있고, 앞산의 이름은 고마高麗산(고구려산)이라고 합니다. 고구려 유민들은 관동지방에 정착하여 고마대권현(高麗大権現)이라는 고구려 대신을 모셨습니다.

② 태일太一문화

칠성문화의 근원으로 들어가서 한번 매듭을 지어보겠습니다. 삼신과 칠성문화의 궁극의 근원은 무엇인가? 이 우주 역사의 진리 주제, 역사의 근본 문제, 원형문화의 원천적 근본 주제가 바로 이것입니다.

우리가 우주 본성, 신의 본성, 우리 생명의 본성, 삶의 목적, 종교의 기도와 수행의 목적 이 모든 것을 한 글자로 축약할 수 있습니다. 『환단고기』의 역사문화의 근본 주제인 밝을 환桓 자, 우주광명 환입니다.

『환단고기』 첫 문장이 무엇입니까? "오환건국吾桓建國이 최고最古라." 오환건국! 우리는 환으로써 나라를 세웠다는 것입니다.

오 환 건 국　　최 고
吾桓建國이 最古라 (「삼성기」 상)

건국, 나라를 어떻게 세울 것인가? 이 우주의 역사와 함께하는, 우주 광명의 심법으로, 우주 광명 인간이 되어서 세운 나라가 창세 환국과 배달과 조선 삼성조입니다. 과거처럼 한 5백 년, 천 년, 몇백 년 하다가 무너지는 그런 나라가 아닙니다. 삼신의 우주 신성을 적당히 깨달은 것이 아니라 그 화신이 되어서 나라를 세웠습니다. 인류 황금시절의 우리 조상들은 스스로 **우주광명 자체 인간, 홍익인간**이 되어서 나라를 세웠습니다. 그것이 최고, 가

After the collapse of the Goguryeo Kingdom in Korea, the Jouiseonin arrived from Goguryeo and established the samurai and Shugendo cultures in Japan. Refugees from Goguryeo pioneered the Kanto region, which included the Tokyo area, and raised horses and practiced martial arts, laying the foundation for the samurai culture. In the Oiso area, there is Goma Shrine, and the mountain in the front is Mt. Gomasan ("Goruryeo Mountain"). The refugees of Goguryeo settled in the Kanto region and worshipped a great deity called 'Goma ("Goguryeo") Daegwonhyeon' ("Great Incarnation").

② Taeil Culture

Let me delve into the root of the Seven Stars culture and draw a conclusion. What is the origin of Samsin and the Seven Stars culture? The central core of cosmic history, the fundamental issue of history, or the basic core of the primordial culture, is the following.

The nature of the universe, of God, and of human life; the purposes of leading life, of religious prayers, and of meditation—all of these can be summarized in one word: *hwan* ("brightness"), which also signifies cosmic radiance. *Hwan* is the key word throughout the history of *Hwandan Gogi*.

What is the first sentence of *Hwandan Gogi*? It is "The state founded by our Hwan people was the most ancient of all states."

> "The state founded by our Hwan people was the most ancient of all states."
> (Source: "Samseong Gi I" of *Hwandan Gogi*)

On the topic of the founding humanity's first states, the Three Sacred Nations—Hwanguk, Baedal, and Joseon—were created, in accordance with the flow of cosmic history, by human beings of cosmic radiance who possessed the mindset of cosmic radiance. Those dynasties were not failing states lasting merely some hundreds of years or a

| 환국 환인천제 | 배달 환웅천황 | 조선 단군왕검 |
| Hwanguk: Heavenly Sovereign Hwanin | Baedal: Heavenly Emperor Hwanung | Joseon: Dangun Wanggeom |

삼신의 신성으로 나라를 세웠던 삼성조 시대
The Three Sacred Nations were built on the basis of Samsin's divinity.

장 오래 되었습니다. 오환건국이 최고라.

우주 경전 「천부경」, 인류 최초의 계시록이면서 첫 경전, 동서 인류의 소
의경전所依經典, 「천부경」 81자. 다 함께 번개처럼 한번 읽어볼까요?

일 시 무 시 일　석 삼 극 무 진 본
상경　一始無始一, 析三極無盡本。

천 일 일 지 일 이 인 일 삼
天一一地一二人一三,

일 적 십 거 무 궤 화 삼
一積十鉅無匱化三。

천 이 삼 지 이 삼 인 이 삼
天二三地二三人二三,

중경　대 삼 합 육 생 칠 팔 구
大三合六生七八九。

운 삼 사 성 환 오 칠
運三四 成環五七。

일 묘 연 만 왕 만 래　용 변 부 동 본
一玅衍 萬往萬來, 用變不動本。

하경　본 심 본 태 양 앙 명
本心本太陽 昂明,

인 중 천 지 일　일 종 무 종 일
人中天地一, 一終無終一。

thousand years as we have witnessed elsewhere in history. The three sacred dynasties were built by those who did not just experience Sam-sin's divinity superficially, but rather had become the embodiment of it on their own. That is, our ancestors who lived during the golden age of humanity built these nations as the human beings of cosmic radiance who fostered wide-reaching benefits for humanity. And the country they built this way was the oldest of all. That is the meaning of the first sentence from *Hwandan Gogi*.

The cosmic scripture *Cheonbu Gyeong ("Scripture of Heavenly Code")* was humanity's first text of revelation, the first scripture, and the fundamental scripture of the peoples of both the East and the West. Shall we quickly read the eighty-one letters of *Cheonbu Gyeong* together?

> Beginning:
> One is the beginning: from Nothingness begins One. One divides into the Three Ultimates, yet the source remains inexhaustible. Arising from One, Heaven is One. Arising from One, Earth is Two. Arising from One, Humanity is Three. One accumulates and opens as Ten, yet all occurs due to Three's creative change.

> Middle:
> Based on Two, Heaven changes under Three. Based on Two, Earth changes under Three. Based on Two, Humanity changes under Three. The Great Three unite into Six, which then gives rise to Seven, Eight, and Nine. Everything moves in accordance with Three and Four; everyting circulates under Five and Seven.

> End:
> One expands in mysterious ways while coming and going endlessly, a great change to the Function occurs, bringing forth immutable Body. The basis of the universe is the mind, which shines radiantly like pure yang. The original mind is fundamentally pure yang, so it shines infinitely. Humanity, penetrating the mind

빨리 읽으면, 마음으로 읽으면 10초밖에 안 걸립니다. 일시무시일一始無始一, 일종무종일一終無終一. 하나에서 비롯됐다가 하나로 돌아갑니다. 그러나 그 시작은 무에서 시작된 하나, 시작이 없는 하나입니다. 이 하나! 이 하나를 위해서 인간은 태어나고 존재하며 죽어갑니다. 그 하나를 위해서, 그 하나를 체험하기 위해서 진리의 궁극, 생명의 근원인 그 하나를 위해서.

일 시 무 시 일
一始無始一

"하나는 절대 존재의 근원이기 때문에 현상화될 수 없다"

일시무시일의 그 하나는 절대 존재의 근원이기 때문에 스스로 현상화될 수가 없습니다. 그래서 석삼극무진본析三極無盡本, 세 가지 지극한 우주의 생명과 신성의 존재로 나타납니다.

석 삼 극 무 진 본
析三極無盡本

"하나는 세 가지 지극한 우주의 생명과 신성으로 나타난다"

그것은 천일天一, 지일地一, 인일人一로 해서 하늘, 땅, 인간 세 가지 지극한 존재의 실제로 나타나지만 그 우주 생명의 궁극 근원은 같습니다. 이것이 인간에 대한 정의입니다! 우리가 살고 있는 대자연 천지부모에 대한 원천적 진리적 신성으로 보는 근본 정의인 것입니다.

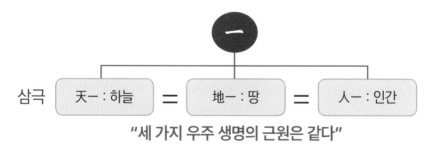

삼극   天一 : 하늘   =   地一 : 땅   =   人一 : 인간

"세 가지 우주 생명의 근원은 같다"

of heaven and earth, attains the Ultimate One. One is the end; in Nothingness ends One.

Giving this a quick read or reviewing it in your heart takes only ten seconds. Concerning the first sentence, things begin from One and return to One. But the beginning is the One that began from Nothingness, the One without beginning. For this One, humans are born, exist, and die for the sake of the One, for experiencing the One, which is also the ultimate truth and the origin of life.

> "One is the root of absolute existence and it cannot be materialized."

Because the One in the phrase "One is the beginning; from Nothingness begins One" is the root of absolute existence, it cannot materialize on its own. Therefore, it manifests as three ultimate cosmic lives or as divinity.

> "One manifests as three ultimate cosmic lives or as divinity."

That is, One manifests as the three ultimates of heaven (Heavenly One), earth (Earthly One), and humanity (Human One), but the origins of these cosmic lives are the same. This is the very definition of humanity. In other words, the basic definition of humanity is that humanity is a fundamentally divine being in relation to nature, wherein humanity lives, or in relation to heaven and earth, humanity's parents.

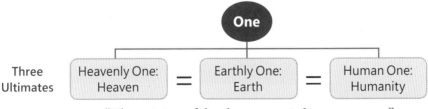

"The origins of the three cosmic lives are same."

그러니까 인간은 무엇인가? 천지의 꿈과 뜻을 완성하는 유일한 궁극의 존재입니다. 그것이 인일ㅅ—인데 나중에 천지의 뜻을 이루기 때문에, 천주의 이상세계를 건설하기 때문에, 점 하나를 쳐서 클 태太 자를 씁니다. 그냥 큰 것이 아니라 태일太—입니다.

이 태일문화는 우리 한국에도 있고 중국에도 살아있는데 태일문화는 정말로 역사문화의 저 그늘진 곳에 가서 숨어 있습니다.

이 문화가 그대로 살아있는 현장이 일본에 있습니다. 스와 호수 남쪽에 신궁이 두 개가 있고, 위쪽에 두 개가 있습니다. 여기에서 일본의 마츠리에서도 아주 유명한 행사가 거행됩니다.

이 태일문화는 솟터에 솟대를 세우는 문화입니다. 저 나가노현(長野縣) 스와시(諏訪市)에 있는 스와(諏訪) 신사의 온바시라 축제, 그 마츠리를 보면 거대한 나무를 깎아 다듬어서 실어오는 것입니다.

스와시의 네 곳에 신사를 둔 스와대사 |
Suwa Grand Shrine complex with four shrines in Suwa City

So, what is humanity? Humanity is the only ultimate being who completes the dream and goal of heaven and earth. That very ultimate being is called Human One. Because Human One is a being who will eventually accomplish the goal of heaven and earth, i.e., build the ideal world of the Lord of Heaven, 'Human' in 'Human One' can be replaced by *tae* ("great") and Human One is then called 'Taeil' ("Great One").

Taeil culture is still alive in Korea and China, but it is hidden in the shadowy eras of history. On the other hand, there are places in Japan where Taeil culture is actively shown. There are two shrines in the south of the Suwa Lake region and two more in the upper area. A large and famous event among all Japanese festivals is held in this region.

This event of Taeil culture involves erecting sacred pillars on elevated sites. At the Onbashira Festival of Suwa Grand Shrine of the city of Suwa, located in Nagano prefecture, participants transport huge trimmed trees.

스와대사 온바시라(솟대) 마츠리 | 신사 네 곳에 모두 16(8×2)개의 신성한 나무를 세운다.
Onbashira ("sacred pillars") Festival in Suwa Grand Shrine
Participants erect a total number of sixteen (8 x 2) sacred pillars in the four shrines.

스와는 무엇인가? 스와는 신라에서 소도문화가 내려간 것입니다. 경상도 사람들이 '세워, 세와, 세와' 하다가 일본식으로 '스와, 스와, 스와'가 되었습니다. 현장에서 들어보면 '스와! 스와! 스와!'인데, '세우라'는 말입니다. 세워, 뭘 세워요? 너의 마음을 세워 봐, 너의 자빠져 있는 가정을 세워 봐, 국가를 세워 봐! 너의 무너진 건강 생명을 세워 봐, 너의 영원한 마음을 세워 봐.

그 함성 속에서 그 문화의 정서를 들어보면서 인류의 축원을 느낄 수 있습니다. 일본은 우리하고 같은 '동포'잖아요? 수많은 젊은이들이 거대한 기둥을 내려오는데, 어떤 때는 깔려서 죽는 경우도 있고 불구가 된 사람들도 꽤 있다고 합니다. 저것을 신사 징문, 본진 바로 옆 좌우에다 두 개를 세우고 그 위쪽에 두 개를 세웁니다. 그 각도를 가만히 보면 북두칠성의 머리, 네 개의 별과 비슷합니다.

Onbashira Festival, Suwa Grand Shrine

What is Suwa? Suwa was the cultural tradition of *sodo*s transmitted from Silla. People in the southeastern provinces of Korea (formerly the area of the Silla Dynasty) said '*sewo*' or, in dialect, '*sewa*,' which means "raise" in Korean, and the pronunciation gradually changed into '*suwa*' in Japan. During festivals in Suwa Grand Shrine, participants shout, "*Suwa, suwa, suwa*," which means "Raise, raise, raise." What can you raise? Raise your mind! Raise your family after any collapse, raise your country! Raise your crumbling health and life! Raise your eternal mind!

When we contemplate the cultural sentiment underlying their shouting, we can feel humanity's prayer. We share an ancestral root with the Japanese, do we not? In the festival, many young participants carry those huge pillars down the mountain, and quite a few of them are said to be crushed, being maimed or even killed. They have two pillars standing on the right and left side of the main building facing the shrine entrance and two more on the corners farther inside. The angle of the four pillars seems to be similar to that of the four stars constituting the 'bowl' of the Big Dipper.

스와대사 온바시라 마츠리
Onbashira Festival, Suwa Grand Shrine

'스와, 스와.' 우리는 세워야 된다! 무너진 역사를 세워야 하며, 잃어버린 문화 원형정신을 세워야 하며, 우리의 뿌리를 잃어버린, 근본을 잃어버린 오늘의 역사정신을 바로 세워야 합니다. 여기에 소도문화의 솟대 세우기의 위대한 정신이 담겨 있는 것입니다.

일본의 태일문화는 이 스와신사로 끝나는가? 그게 아닐 것입니다. 일본 역사문화의 진국은 뒷골목을 가봐야 됩니다. 스와신사에 소속된 신사가 또 하나 있었습니다. 여기에 천지비밀이 있습니다.

해가 떨어지려고 하는데 '빨리 가자' 해서 그 옆 마을로 쭉 올라가는데 거기에 신사 하나가 있었습니다. 한번 볼까요?

솟대를 세우는 온바시라御柱 마츠리 |
The Onbashira Festival, raising sacred pillars

Suwa, suwa. We have to raise the fallen history, the lost primordial culture and its spirit, and our present sense of history that has lost our root and origin. That is what the great spirit of raising sacred pillars in the *sodo* culture is all about.

Is Suwa Grand Shrine all of Japanese Taeil culture? That would not be the case. To see genuine Japanese culture, you should visit back-streets. In fact, there is another shrine affiliated with Suwa Grand Shrine. A secret of heaven and earth is hidden in that shrine.

It was at about sunset, so we rushed through a nearby village and ran into a shrine. Shall we take a look at it?

태일사 입구
The entrance of Taeil Shrine

　여기가 태일사泰一寺인데, 2백 개의 아주 가파른 계단으로 아주 조심스럽게 불을 밝히면서 올라갔습니다. 그런데 이 태일사를 지키는 주인공은, 저 왼쪽에 있는 비문 뒤를 보니까 바로 모노노베(物部) 집안 후손들입니다. 그러니까 불교에 저항하며 토속신, 천신 숭배, 소도문화를 지키려 했던 모노노베의 후손들이 이 태일사를 대대로 지켜온 것입니다.

태일사의 제주祭主, 모노노베 야스사다物部安貞
Ritual Host of Taeil Shrine:
Mononobe Yasusada

　그 동네 입구를 가보면 '여기가 바로 태일사다'라는 간판이 있습니다. 제가 그것을 보고서 '아, 모든 피로가 다 풀리는구나. 일본 역사문화의 비밀이, 신라 역사의 비밀이 여기에 있구나. 우리 단군조선, 그 이전 환국, 배달의 역사문화의 우주정신이 바로 여기에 있구나' 하고 크게 감동을 한 적이 있습니다.

환국·배달·단군조선의 역사, 문화 정신이 살아있는 일본 태일사
The historical and cultural spirit of Hwanguk, Baedal, and Dangun Joseon is still alive in Japan's Taeil Shrine.

This is Taeil Shrine. We cautiously went up two hundred steep stairs, shining a light. The guardians of Taeil Shrine were, according to the inscription on the back of the stone monument standing on the left, the descendants of the Mononobe Clan. In other words, the descendants of the Mononobe Clan who intended to guard local deities, the worship of Heavenly God, and the *sodo* culture against Buddhism have been safeguarding Taeil Shrine for generations.

At the village entrance, there is a sign saying: "This is Taeil Shrine." Seeing that sign, I felt as if all my fatigue had melted away, and I was deeply touched by the thought: "The secrets of Japanese history and those of Silla's history can be found right here in this shrine. And the historical spirit of Dangun Joseon, and that of Baedal and Hwanguk before Dangun Joseon, endure in this very shrine."

그러면 우리 조선시대에는 태일문화가 없었을까요? 창덕궁昌德宮을 들어가서 보면 연경당演慶堂 태일문太一門이 있습니다. 이것을 사진 찍어서 『환단고기』 완역본 해설에 넣은 적이 있습니다. 지금은 태일문을 숨겨서 보지 못하게 하고 안으로 걸어 잠가 버렸습니다.

우리나라에 '칼을 든 유학자' 남명南冥 조식曺植(1501~1572)이라는 분이 퇴계退溪 이황李滉(1501~1570) 선생과 음양 쌍을 이룹니다. 벼슬을 안 하고 초야에 묻혀 살던 남명 선생이 '태일은 모든 진리, 천지도덕의 근본이요 중심'이라 써놓았습니다. 우주 생명, 신성, 도덕, 진리, 궁극의 인간상 그게 태일이라는 겁니다. 이렇게 태일을 안 유학자가 있었어요. 태일을 조선의 왕도문화로 알았던 것입니다.

태일문 | 창덕궁 연경당
조선시대에도 태일문화가 있었다.

Taeil Gate
Yeongyeongdang House, Changdeokgung Palace
The Joseon Dynasty also had Taeil culture.

Then, was there not Taeil culture in the Joseon Dynasty in Korea? In the Changdeokgung Palace complex, there is the Taeil Gate in Yeongyeongdang House. I added a picture of this gate to the commentary of *Hwandan Gogi*. Currently, this Taeil Gate is locked and hidden from the public.

Jo Sik (1501-1572; pen name: 'Nammyeong') was a Confucian scholar who used to carry a sword at his waist. He and Yi Hwang (1501-1570; pen name: 'Toegye') were two great authorities in the field of Confucian studies during the Joseon Dynasty and can be likened to yin and yang. Living in seclusion without holding public office, Jo Sik left a written passage: "Taeil is the foundation and center of all the truths and morals of heaven and earth." That is, Taeil signifies cosmic life, divinity, morality, truth, and the ultimate image of the ideal human being. This conception of Taeil by Jo Sik, a Confucian scholar, meant that he recognized Taeil as the principle of royalty in Joseon Dynasty.

남명 조식曺植 | 1501~1572
Jo Sik
(pen name: 'Nammyeong';
1501-1572)

신명사도神明舍圖 | 심성수양의 요체를 표현한 그림
Jo Sik's Sinmyeongsado Diagram showing key
factors in the cultivation of the mind

다시 일본으로 가볼까요? 일본 10만 개 신사의 원 사령탑인 이세신궁伊勢神宮, 태양 하나님을 모시고 있는 그 내궁이 태일문화를 깔고 있습니다. 내궁의 문양은 북두칠성을 닮았고, 외궁을 보면 수레 문양이 태일신의 수레 역할을 하는 북두칠성을 상징 합니다.

중국을 보면 『환단고기』에도 한 구절이 나오듯이 사마상여司馬相如가 한 무제에게 "폐하는 겸양하시어, 봉선封禪을 행하기 위해 출발하지 않으신다." 했는데 이것은 상제님을 잘 모시라는 것입니다. 정치를 하려면 우주정치를 행하시는 천상의 상제님을 잘 받들라는 말입니다.

上帝垂恩 … 陛下謙讓 …。
상제수은   폐하겸양

사마상여가 한 무제에게 '겸양'하여 상제님을 잘 모실 것을 권함

(『사기』「사마상여열전」)

그리고 사마천司馬遷의 『사기史記』「봉선서封禪書」를 보면, 천일·지일·태일신에서 태일신이 가장 높기 때문에, 가장 존귀한 신성이기 때문에 한무제가 궁궐 동남방에다가 태일전太一殿을 세우고 천제를 올렸다는 구절이 있습니다.

이세신궁 내궁문양 | 태일신 궁전 상징
The pattern of the inner shrine at Ise Grand Shrine symbolizes the Taeil Spirit's palace.

Shall we return to Japan? The Ise Grand Shrine is the original leader of a hundred thousand Japanese Shinto shrines, and its inner shrine, dedicated to the sun god, has a trace of Taeil culture. The pattern of the inner shrine resembles the Big Dipper, and the wagon pattern of the outer shrine symbolizes the Big Dipper, which serves as the Taeil Spirit's wagon.

In the case of China, as mentioned in a passage of *Hwandan Gogi*, Sima Xiangru said to Emperor Wu of the Han Dynasty, "Your Majesty, you have been too humble and have not set out to conduct offering rituals to heaven and earth." This meant that he should have served Sangjenim attentively. That is, to assume the helm of the state, the ruler should properly serve Sangjenim in heaven, who governs the universe.

> "Sangjenim bestows his grace…His Majesty is humble…"
> (Source: "Biography of Sima Xiangru" *Records of the Grand Historian*)

Sima Xiangru meant that Emperor Wu of Han was humble and that the emperor should have served Sangjenim with great care.

이세신궁 외궁문양 | 태일신의 수레(북두칠성) 상징
The pattern of the outer shrine at Ise Grand Shrine symbolizes the wagon of the Taeil Spirit (the Big Dipper).

그리고 일본에는 막부의 마지막 장군, 도쿠가와 이에야스의 손자가 할아버지를 존경해서 신사를 만들었다가 나중에 동조궁東照宮으로 바꾸었습니다. 거기를 가보면 『환단고기』 우주광명 문화의 비밀이 다 잠들어 있습니다.

　그리고 우리의 전통 상투 문화가 바로 이 우주의 태일문화입니다. 내 몸에 우주의 생명과 신성과 진리와 영원한 마음, 도통 마음, 솟대를 세우는 것입니다. 우리 머리 위에다가 '나는 우주의 통치자, 우주 생명의 원주인인 삼신상제님과 한마음으로 산다'는 뜻으로 상투를 틉니다. 그것이 바로 내 마음에 세우는 내 몸의 소도, 상투인 것입니다.

일본 동조궁東照宮 |
Tosho-gu in Japan

And in the "Treatises on Sacrifice" of Sima Qian's *Records of the Grand Historian*, there is a passage explaining that since the Taeil Spirit is a higher and nobler divine being than Cheonil ("Heavenly One") Spirit and Ji-il ("Earthly One") Spirit, Emperor Wu of Han Dynasty had Taeil Hall built southeast of his palace to offer heavenly rituals. In Japan, the grandson of Tokugawa Ieyasu, a ruler of the last feudal government in Japan, had a Shinto shrine built out of respect for his grandfather, and this shrine was later changed into Tosho-gu ("Shrine of the Light of the East"). In this shrine, the secrets of the cosmic radiance culture of *Hwandan Gogi* are sleeping.

The traditional Korean custom of tying a topknot is a form of Taeil culture. Tying a topknot was an act of establishing the cosmic life, divinity, eternal mind, enlightened mind, and a sacred pole in one's body. People in the past tied a topknot on their head in the belief that they shared one mind with Samsin Sangjenim, who is the Ruler of the Universe and the original master of cosmic life. That is, the topknot was the sacred pole of one's body, and it was also erected in one's mind.

③ 삼신三神문화

신라의 삼신문화는 이 지구의 문화를 소통시킨 유목문화의 근본정신인 삼신칠성 문화, 용봉문화, 그리고 도깨비 문화입니다.

나라를 셋으로 나누어 다스리는 단군조선의 삼한관경제는 지구촌 문화의 근원이 됩니다.

삼국유사 제1권 기이편에 등장하는 이야기.

신라의 삼신상제 문화를 보여주는 예*가 있습니다. 진평왕眞平王 즉위 첫 해에 천상에서 천사가 내려와서 '이것은 상제님이 내려주시는 옥대玉帶다. 이걸 받아라' 해서 진평왕이 받아서 찼다는 것입니다. 이 옥대가 신라 호국 삼보의 하나입니다.

그 다음에 표훈表訓(?~?)이라는 분이 신교사상에 정통하여 삼신오제의 원리를 투철히 깨쳤습니다. 이분은 『환단고기』 첫 편을 쓴 안함로와 더불어서 신라 10대 성인의 한 사람입니다.

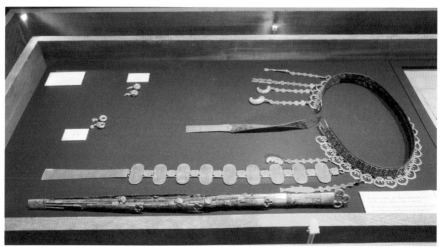

옥대玉帶 | 진평왕이 상제님께 하사받음. 신라 호국 삼보의 하나. 국립경주박물관
Jade belt: Bestowed upon King Jinpyeong by Sangjenim.
One of three Silla treasures for the protection of the nation. (Collection of Gyeongju National Museum)

③ Samsin Culture

The Samsin culture of the Silla Dynasty demonstrated the cultural traditions of: Samsin and the Seven Stars; the dragon and phoenix; *dokkaebi* (goblin-like beings), which are the fundamental spirits of the nomad culture that enabled cross-cultural communication in the global village. The system of the Territory of Jurisdiction Partitioned into Three Han States during the Dangun Joseon era, a system that divided the country into three regions for governance, created the basis for the cultures of the global village.

Here is an example that demonstrates the Samsin Sangjenim culture of the Silla Dynasty. A narrative* asserts that in the first year of King Jinpyeong's reign, an angel descended from heaven and said to the king,

> **narrative**. This narrative is in chapter one "Wonder" in *Samguk Yusa*.

"This is a jade belt granted by Sangjenim. Receive it." So, the king is said to have accepted the belt and worn it. This was one of three Silla treasures for the protection of the nation.

In Silla, there was also a person named 'Pyohun' (?-?), who was conversant with Spirit Teaching and thus possessed profound knowledge about the principle of Samsin and the Five Emperors. Together with An-

hamro, who wrote the first chapter of *Hwandan Gogi*, that is, *Samseong Gi I*, Pyohun is one of the ten venerable Buddhist monks of Silla.

표훈表訓 대덕 | ?~?. 안함로(『삼성기』 상 저자)와 함께 신라 10대 성인에 속함
Venerable Monk Pyohun
Together with Anhamro (the author of *Samseong Gi I*), he is one of the ten venerable Buddhist monks of Silla.

신라의 35세 경덕왕景德王은 표훈에게 '나는 아들이 없으니까, 자네가 천상 상제님께 가서 아들을 내려 달라고 빌어라'라고 했습니다. 그리하여 상제님께 가서 비니까 '안 된다. 딸밖에 못 준다'라고 했는데, 다시 상제님께 '딸을 아들로 바꿔 달라'는 사연을 고하니까, '아들이 내려가면 나라가 위태로울 것'이라 했습니다. 그래도 경덕왕은 그 아들을 받았고 아들은 후에 36세 혜공왕惠恭王이 되었는데, 여자놀이를 하고 여자처럼 행동했다고 합니다.

　환국·배달·조선·북부여 이후에 이런 우주 원형문화, 우주광명 문화, 신교 삼신문화가 있었습니다. 왕의 옆에 있던 도승들이 삼신상제님의 천상 궁전을 오르내린 야사 같은 이야기가 사서에 엄연히 기록되어 있는 것입니다.

　신라는 신교라고 하는, 7천 년 삼신칠성 우주 원형문화를 가지고 있었습니다. 신라는 박물관에 가 봐도 알 수 있듯이 도깨비 문화의 원형을 그대로 가지고 있습니다.

According to a story, King Gyeongdeok, the thirty-fifth ruler of the Silla Dynasty, who had no son, asked Pyohun to go to Sangjenim in heaven and appeal to Sangjenim to grant the king a son. Thus, Pyohun ascended to Sangjenim and begged him to grant the king's wish. Sangjenim answered that he would not bless the king with a son, but a daughter. Then Pyohun went to Sangjenim again to convey the king's request to change the daughter into a son. Sangjenim warned that if a son were granted, the country would be faced with a perilous situation. The king nevertheless accepted the risk and received a son, who later became King Hyegong, the thirty-sixth ruler of Silla. By the way, the son is said to have acted like a girl and enjoyed girlish games.

The primordial culture of the universe, the culture of cosmic radiance, and Spirit Teaching's Samsin culture continued to exist after the eras of Hwanguk, Baedal, Dangun Joseon, and Northern Buyeo. Against this backdrop, stories like an unofficial history in which enlightened Buddhist monks serving the kings ascended to Samsin Sangjenim's palace in heaven and came back were clearly recorded in history texts. Silla possessed Spirit Teaching, which was the primordial culture of the universe and the cultural tradition of Samsin and the Seven Stars, and which lasted some seven thousand years. As shown in museum collections, Silla also possessed the original form of *dokkaebi* (goblin-like beings) culture.

제3장

통일문화를 여는
근대사의 새 울림

 오늘 말씀의 마무리는 '통일문화를 여는 근대사의 새 울림'인데 간명하게 핵심만 정리하고 마무리를 짓겠습니다.

년도	신라의 삼국통일 과정	중국
법흥왕(532)	금관가야를 합병 ⇒김유신의 조부인 김무력은 신라의 장군이 됨	
진흥왕(554)	관산성 전투로 나제동맹이 파기됨 ⇒김무력은 신흥귀족 지위 확보	위진남북조시대
선덕여왕(642)	백제장군 윤충이 김춘추의 맏사위 품석과 큰딸 고타소를 죽임	당 태종
무열왕(655)	김춘추가 당나라에 군사원조 요청	
무열왕(660)	나·당 연합군이 백제 함락	당고종 측천무후
문무왕(668)	나·당 연합군이 고구려 함락	

Chapter 3

A New Movement of Modern History to Initiate a Culture of Unification

The theme of today's conclusion is: a new movement of modern history to initiate a unified culture. I will conclude today's lecture by simply summarizing the key points of what has been said so far.

Year	The Unification Process of the Three Kingdoms by Silla	China
King Beopheung (532)	Silla absorbed Geumgwan Gaya, and Gim Yusin's grandfather, Gim Muryeok, who was of the royal blood of Geumgwan Gaya, became a general of Silla.	Wei, Jin, Northern and Southern Dynasties
King Jinheung (554)	The Silla-Baekje alliance was broken due to the battle for Gwansan-seong Fortress. Gim Muryeok rose, becoming new nobility.	
Queen Seondeok (642)	Baekje General Yun Chung captured and executed Gotaso and Gim Pumseok, who were Gim Chunchu's first daughter and first son-in-law respectively.	Tang Dynasty: Emperor Taizong
King Muyeol (655)	Gim Chunchu requested military aid from the Tang Dynasty.	Tang Dynasty: Emperor Gaozong and Empress Wu Zetian
King Muyeol (660)	The allied forces of Silla and Tang captured Baekje.	
King Munmu (668)	The allied forces of Silla and Tang captured Goguryeo.	

신라의 27세 선덕여왕善德女王, 28세 진덕여왕眞德女王, 그 다음에 백제를 멸망시키고 세상을 떠나는 김춘추金春秋, 즉 무열왕武烈王이 나왔습니다.

그런데 무열왕 김춘추와 김유신金庾信(595~673)은 자신들의 어떤 개인적 원한으로 인하여 백제를 멸망시키고 고구려를 공격 했습니다. 김유신은 전생에 고구려의 유명한 점쟁이 추남이었다고 합니다. 국경 지방에 홍수가 나서 고구려왕이 그 이유를 묻자 추남은 '왕비마마가 부정을 저지른 일 때문이다'라고 대답을 했습니다. 그 답변으로 추남의 목숨이 위태로워졌을 게 아닙니까? 다음에는 생쥐를 갖다놓고 보이지 않게 가린 뒤 점을 쳐서 몇 마리인지 알아맞히게 했습니다. 추남은 여덟 마리라고 답했습니다. 그러자 '이놈이 쥐 한 마리를 여덟 마리라고 잘못 맞추었다'고 추남을 사형시켰는데, 그는 죽으면서 '내가 훗날 장군으로 태어나서 고구려를 멸망시킬 것이다'라고 했습니다. 나중에 쥐의 배를 갈라보니까 새끼 일곱 마리가 들어있었나는 이야기가 『삼국유사』에 있습니다.

김춘추는 사위 김품석과 딸이 대야성 전투에서 백제의 윤충에게 죽었습니다. 그런데 원래 그 사위가 검일의 처를 겁탈했는데 검일이 그 원한으로 백제군과 내통해서 대야성을 공격하게 했습니다. 김춘추는 딸과 사위가 목숨을 잃자, 넋을 놓고 사람이 지나가도 모르고 온종일 울었다고 합니다.

『환단고기』를 보면 김춘추가 고구려에 가서 연개소문淵蓋蘇文을 만났습니다. 연개소문이 '우리가 당나라를 멸망시키고 그 땅을 나누어서 함께 다스리자'고 제안했는데, 김춘추는 그것을 받아들이지 않고 돌아왔습니다. 그러고서 김춘추는 당나라에 자기 둘째 아들 김인문金仁問을 보냈습니다. 김인문은 40년 동안 당나라 조정에서 있으면서 당태종과 당고종의 호감을 샀습니다. 그렇게 신라가 당과의 외교를 중시했는데 나중에 김인문이 죽어서 시신이 돌아오자 왕이 예를 갖추어 제를 지냈습니다.

Silla's twenty-seventh ruler, Queen Seondeok, was succeeded by the twenty-eighth, Queen Jindeok, and then Gim Chunchu was crowned as King Muyeol, who destroyed Baekje during his reign.

By the way, Gim Chunchu (King Muyeol) and Gim Yusin (595-673) might have destroyed Baekje and attacked Goguryeo out of a personal grudge. According to a story, Gim Yusin was, in a past life, Chunam, a famous fortune-teller in Goguryeo. When a border region was flooded, the king of Goguryeo asked him why, and Chunam answered that the flood resulted from the queen's unfaithfulness. This answer endangered his life. Then he was ordered to guess the number of mice shielded from his sight. His answer was eight, but there was only one that was hidden before him. So the king ordered him executed for making a wrong guess. When he was about to be executed, Chunam cried out that he would be reborn as a general in another country and destroy his home country, Goguryeo. After his death, seven pups were found when the mouse's belly was cut open. This story is from *Samguk Yusa*.

In the case of Gim Chunchu, his daughter and his son-in-law, Gim Pumseok, were killed by Baekje general Yun Chung during the battle of Daeya-seong Fortress. Before the battle, Gim Pumseok took his subordinate Geomil's wife by force, incurring his enmity, and the vindictive Geomil secretly entered into league with Baekje to aid its attack on Daeya-seong Fortress.

Grief-stricken, Gim Chunchu was so absentminded that he could not even notice people near him and wept bitterly all day long.

According to *Hwandan Gogi*, Gim Chunchu visited Goguryeo and met Goguryeo's leader, Yeon Gaesomun. Yeon Gaesomun proposed combining the forces of the two countries to destroy the Tang Dynasty and then divide that land, but Gim Chunchu returned to Silla without concluding the deal. Later, Gim Chunchu sent his second son, Gim Inmun, to the Tang Dynasty. Gim Inmun held a government post in the Tang Dynasty for forty years and won the favor of Emperor Taizong

신라는 진덕여왕 때부터 왕과 벼슬아치가 당나라 관복을 입고 중국 연호를 사용하기 시작했습니다. 또 김춘추는 화랑도가 자발적으로 국가에 충성을 바치는 집단이기 때문에, 체계적인 국가 운영의 인력 집단으로 활용하는 데에는 한계가 있다고 생각했습니다. 화랑도는 왕이 인재를 체계적으로 직접 뽑고, 기르고, 씀으로써 국력을 진작하고 왕권을 강화하는 제도에 적합하지 않았습니다. 그래서 당나라의 국가 경영제도 국학國學을 수용했습니다. 그러면서 급속히 당나라 중심의 사대주의 역사의식으로 기울어졌습니다.

그러면 신라에서 왜 당나라를 끌어들여서 형제 국가를 멸망시켰는가? 수나라, 당나라를 선비족이 세웠고, **신라 김씨 왕족은 바로 훈족, 흉노족이었습니다.** 이처럼 신라는 북방 유목문화와 친연성親緣性이 있기 때문에 당나라와의 대화가 잘된 것입니다. 그리고 그 외에 국가 이권 문제도 여럿 있었을 것입니다.

이 삼국통일의 한계는 무엇인가? 신라와 백제는 북부여 왕조에서 나왔고 당나라는 북방 유목민이 세웠으므로, 신라와 당의 문화 친연성은 얼마든지 인정할 수 있습니다. 그러나 신라는 자기의 본래 큰집, 즉 고구려를 공격하여 멸망시켜버린 겁니다.

and Gaozong of Tang. Silla valued diplomatic relations with Tang this highly. When Gim Inmun died in Tang, his body was returned to Silla, and the Silla king courteously held a memorial service.

The King of Silla and government officials started wearing the Tang Dynasty's official uniform and using its era name beginning in the time of Queen Jindeok. And Gim Chunchu understood the limitations of utilizing the Hwarang Knights as a state-managed manpower source because it was a voluntary group loyal to their country. That is, it was not suitable to serve as a system wherein the king directly selected, cultivated, and appointed competent people, boosting national power and strengthening royal authorities. Thus, Silla adopted Gukhak ("National Academy"), the Tang Dynasty's system.

Then the historical consciousness of Silla people rapidly tilted toward Tang-centric flunkeyism.

By the way, what led Silla to draw upon the Tang Dynasty in order to destroy its brother countries? In fact, both the Tang Dynasty and its predecessor, the Sui Dynasty, were established by Xianbei, and Silla's royal family, the Gim Clan, were the Huns (Xiongnu). Because Silla had such an affinity with the northern nomad cultures, its negotiation with the Tang Dynasty seems to have progressed well. Also, there would have been national interests involved.

What was the second limitation of the Three Kingdoms' unification by Silla? Because Silla and Baekje originated from the Northern Buyeo Dynasty, and the Tang Dynasty was established by northern nomads, the cultural affinity between Silla and Tang was totally understandable. But after all, Silla destroyed the original house of its royal family—that is, Goguryeo.

신라 삼국통일의 한계

1. 외세(당나라)를 끌어들여 형제국가(백제, 고구려)를 멸망시킴
2. 신라가 큰집(고구려)을 멸망시킴

고구려는 본래 북방의 진국辰國, 바로 진한辰韓입니다. 고구려가 패망하자 고구려의 장수 대중상大仲象과 그 아들 대조영大祚榮이 새로 나라를 세우고 '우리가 진국이다, 후고구려다' 라고 주장하며, 단군조선의 북방 진한의 역사와 문화 정신을 그대로 계승했습니다. 그리하여 또 하나의 천자국, '살아 있는 후고구려'가 나온 것입니다. 대진大震 즉 발해渤海는 통치자를 황제라 부른 천자국입니다.

그런데 신라와 대진 이 두 나라는 남북으로 대치하는 적대국이 되었습니다. 고운孤雲 최지원이 쓴 글에 새미나는 일화가 있습니다. 대진국의 유학생이 당나라의 시험에서 수석을 한 적이 있는데 그때 최치원이 이를 못마땅히 여겨서 '촌놈이 하나 와서 운좋게 수석을 했다'라고 평했다는 것입니다.

북방의 대진은 그 역사 자체가 『삼국사기』에 없지만, 그 사람들이 환국·배달의 삼신오제三神五帝 문화를 그대로 가지고 수도를 오경五京으로 만들었습니다.

Limitation of the Three Kingdoms' Unification by Silla

1. By drawing upon foreign influence (the Tang Dynasty), Silla destroyed its brother countries (Baekje and Goguryeo).
2. Silla destroyed the original house of its royal family (Goguryeo).

Goguryeo originated from the Jin State in the northern region—that is, Jinhan. When Goguryeo collapsed, a Goguryeo general, Dae Jungsang, and his son, Dae Joyeong, became the inheritors of the historical and cultural spirit of Jinhan, the northern wing of Dangun Joseon, proclaiming that—since it had its roots in the Jin State—their new country was 'Later Goguryeo.' That is how another state of the Son of Heaven, the 'living' Later Goguryeo, came into being. Daejin, also known as 'Balhae,' was a state of the Son of Heaven in which the ruler was called 'Emperor.'

However, the two countries of Silla and Daejin became adversaries, confronting each other in the north and south. There is an interesting anecdote in a text by Choe Chiwon (pen name: 'Goun'), a renowned Silla scholar. It asserts that when a student from Daejin attained the top standing in a state exam in Tang, Choe Chiwon ridiculed the Daejin student's achievement, saying that the bumpkin had attained first place by sheer luck. The history of Daejin, a northern state, does not even exist in the records of *Samguk Sagi*, but the people of Daejin established five capitals based on the tradition of Samsin and the Five Emperors from Hwanguk and Baedal.

서경압록부
상경용천부
대진(발해)
중경현덕부
동경용원부
남경남해부
북원경
서원경
통일신라
중원경
남원경
금관경
환국·배달의 삼신오제五帝문화에 따라
수도를 오경五京으로 설치함

　신라도 통일 후에 오경을 설치하여 국가를 경영했습니다. 그런데 서울대
교수나 일반 학자들이 쓴 논문의 결론은 무엇인가? 그 오경은 중국의 오행
사상으로 만들었다는 것입니다. 그러나 그게 아닙니다.

　『환단고기』를 보면 우주의 시간 공간의 원형사상 구조, 동서남북 중앙
오령五靈 사상, 오제五帝 사상에 의해서 그런 오방五方, 오경제도가 나온 것을
알 수 있습니다.

Western Capital
Amnok

Upper Capital
Yongcheon

Daejin
(Balhae)

Central Capital
Hyeondeok

Eastern Capital
Yongwon

Southern Capital
Namhae

Unified Silla

Secondary Capital
in Bukwon

Secondary Capital
in Seowon

Secondary Capital
in Jungwon

According to the culture of Samsin and
Five Emperors (which originated from
Hwanguk and Baedal), Daejin and
Unified Silla established five capitals.

Secondary Capital
in Namwon

Secondary Capital
in Geumgwan

After unification with its two rivals, Silla also administered the country based on a five secondary capital system. By the way, do you know what a Seoul National University professor and other scholars wrote concerning the five secondary capitals of Unified Silla? They claimed in their theses that Silla's five secondary capital system was based on China's theory of five elements. That is not true. *Hwandan Gogi* shows that the concept of five directions and the five secondary capital system developed from the theory of: the universe's original structure of time and space; the Five Spirits located in the east, west, south, north, and center respectively; and the Five Emperors.

신교의 부활, 동학과 참동학

신라 천년 왕도 경주, 이 경주가 고대사뿐만 아니라 근대사에서 얼마나 진정한 역사 성지인가?

신라의 정신문화 원형을 세워 준 분은 누구인가? 그분은 바로 경주 최씨 소벌도리의 후손 최치원으로, 우주경전 「천부경」을 해석해서 후세에 전해 주었습니다. 그리고 이분이 '국유현묘지도國有玄妙之道 왈풍류曰風流라', "우리나라에 아주 현묘한, 어떤 지식이나 유교, 불교, 도교로 알 수 없는 아주 깊고 신비스러운 도가 있으니 풍류風流라 한다"라고 하였습니다.

국 유 현 묘 지 도 　 왈 풍 류
國有玄妙之道 曰風流。

유교·불교·도교로는 알 수 없는 오묘하고 신비한 도가 있는데 풍류風流라 이른다. (『삼국사기』「난랑비서문」)

즉, 신의 조화의 진리 가르침이 있다'는 것입니다. 그것을 신교라 하고 신도라고도 하는데, 일본이 그것을 따다가 국가종교 신도를 만든 것입니다.

그리고 진정한 통일문화 시대를 선언한 새로운 성인이 바로 이 경주에서 마침내 나타났습니다. 그분이 바로 최제우입니다. 최고운의 후손 최수운 대신사입니다.

최치원崔致遠 | 857~?.
경주 최씨의 중시조. 소벌도리의 24세손
Choe Chiwon (857- ?):
A twenty-fourth generation descendant of
Sobeoldori, he revived the fame of the Choe Clan
from Gyeongju.

The Revival of Spirit Teaching, Eastern Learning, and True Eastern Learning

What a genuine sacred land of Korea's ancient and modern history Gyeongju is—the capital of Silla for nearly a thousand years! Who established the prototype of Silla's spiritual culture? That was Choe Chiwon, a descendant of Sobeoldori, who interpreted the cosmic scripture *Cheonbu Gyeong* and passed it down to posterity. He wrote: "In our country, there is an esoteric and mysterious dao (that cannot be understood by means of Confucinism, Buddhism, or Daoism). It is called *pungnyu*."

> "In our country, there is an esoteric and mysterious dao (that cannot be understood by means of Confucianism, Buddhism, or Daoism). It is called *pungnyu*."
> [Source: Preface to Nannangbi ("Inscription on the tomb of Knight Nan") *Samguk Sagi*]

The writing signifies that there is a true teaching of God's creation-transformation. This is called 'Spirit Teaching' or 'Spirit Dao.' Japan adopted Spirit Teaching and derived their national religion, Shinto, from it.

Later, a new sage finally emerged here in Gyeongju, and it was he

who declared the era of unified culture in the true sense. He was Choe Je-u (aka, 'Choe Su-un'), a descendant of the renowned scholar Choe Chiwon (pen name: 'Goun').

수운 최제우崔濟愚 | 1824~1864
최치원의 25세손. 동학東學 창도(1860)
Choe Je-u (pen name: 'Su-un') (1824-1864)
A twenty-fifth generation descendant of Choe Chiwon.
Established Eastern Learning in 1860.

그러면 이분은 어떤 분인가? 김범부金凡夫(1897~1966)라는 분이 '얼마나 위대한지 아느냐' 하고 아주 이런 멋진 언사를 썼습니다.

"경신년 4월 5일에 정말 어마어마한 역사적 대사건이 경주에서 발생했다. 수운 최제우는 천계天啓를 받았다는 것이다. 이것이 과연 '역사적 대강령大降靈'이며 동시에 '신도성시神道盛時 정신의 기적적 부활'이라 할 것이다. '국풍國風의 재생'이라 할 것이며, '사태史態의 경이'라 할 것이다."

'수운 최제우는 천계天啓를 받았다.'
'이것은 인류의 새 문화역사를 여는 대강령이며 신도성시神道盛時 정신의 기적적 부활이며 국풍國風의 재생이며 사태史態의 경이로다.' (범부 김정설, 『최제우론』)

다시 말하자면, 최수운 대신사가 1860년 음력 4월 5일 날, 마투 우주 징치, 우주 역사를 주관하시는, 9천 년 인류가 신성한 땅 소도에서 섬겨온 소도제천의 주인공 삼신상제님과 직접 대화를 나누면서 천명을 받은 기적의 순간이 경주 용담정龍潭亭에서 일어났는데 이는 인류 역사에서 대사건이라는 것입니다.

범부 김정설金鼎卨 | 1897~1966. 동양철학자
저서 『최제우론』 외
Gim Jeong-seol (pen name: 'Beombu'; 1897-1966)
A scholar of Eastern philosophy.
Authored *Discourse on Choe Je-u*, etc.

Who was Choe Je-u? A scholar, Gim Jeong-seol (pen name: 'Beombu'; 1897-1966), presented the following wonderful remarks concerning Choe Je-u's greatness: "On the fifth day of the fourth month, 1860, a truly amazing historical event took place in Gyeongju, and the event was that Choe Je-u received a revelation from God. This was indeed a 'historically great descent of God's Holy Spirit' and a 'miraculous resurrection of the mindset from Spirit Teaching's golden era,' 'a revival of national customs,' and a 'marvelous historic event.'"

> "... Choe Je-u received a revelation from God."
> "This was indeed a 'historically great descent of God's Holy Spirit' and a 'miraculous resurrection of the mindset from Spirit Teaching's golden era,' 'a revival of national customs,' and a 'marvelous historic event.'"
> (Source: *Discourse on Choe Je-u* by Gim Jeong-seol)

To sum up what he meant, miraculous moments occurred in Yongdamjeong House, Gyeongju, on the fifth day of the fourth lunar month in 1860, and what happened in those moments was that the Sacred Venerable Choe Je-u had dialogues with, and received a heavenly mandate from, Samsin Sangjenim, the one who supervises cosmic politics and history, and the one who was the object of worship in heavenly rituals held at *sodo*s, sacred land, by humanity for about nine thousand years.

용담정龍潭亭 | 경주시 구미산
Yongdamjeong House
Location: Mt. Gumisan,
Gyeongju

이때 받은 메시지를 크게 세 가지로 볼 수 있는데, 그것은 무엇인가?

'십이제국 괴질운수 다시개벽 아닐런가', '호천금궐 상제님을 너희 어찌 알까보냐', '나를 아버지로 불러라' 입니다.

최수운이 상제님에게 받은 메시지

"십이제국 괴질운수 다시개벽 아닐런가." (『용담유사』)

"호천금궐 상제님을 너희 어찌 알까보냐." (『용담유사』)

"나를 아버지로 부르도록 하라." (『도원기서』)

예수는 아버지가 보내서 온 아들입니다. '이는 나의 사랑하는 아들이다' 라는 말과 함께, 비둘기 성령 계시가 내려왔다고 합니다.

그런데 _ 이 아버지가 동방 땅에서 완전히 다른 새로운 우주 역사를 여시기 위해서, 동학을 열게 하신 것입니다. 그 가르침을 살펴보면, 십이제국에 이름을 알 수 없는 괴질병이 앞으로 지구촌을 강타하면서 지나온 선천문명은 다 무너지고 새로운 우주시대, 새로운 우주질서가 열린다는 것입니다. '다시 개벽'이다 이겁니다. 이런 개벽사상과, 우주정치의 주인공 상제님이 앞으로 오신다는 것을 선포했습니다.

그때 '주문을 받아라. 이것으로써 천하창생을 가르쳐라' 하고 내려주신 것이, 열석 자 '시천주 조화정 영세불망만사지'입니다. 이 **시천주**侍天主가 왜 곡이 되어서 지금 뭐가 됐어요? 시천주가 **인내천**人乃天이 된 것입니다. 동학이 왜곡되어서 천도교天道敎가 되었습니다. 모든 교과서, 대학 교과서에 전부 이렇게 왜곡돼서 근대 역사의 첫 출발점, 이 위대한 경주에서의 새 세상 소식이, 새 역사 선언 내용이 누구도 본질을 알 수 없게 된 것입니다.

The overall messages that Choe Je-u received were three. They were: "The fate of the mysterious disease spreading across the entire world—is this not once again *gaebyeok*?", "How could you possibly know Sangjenim of Heaven's Golden Palace?", "Call me your father."

Messages that Choe Je-u received from Sangjenim:

"The fate of the mysterious disease spreading across the entire world—is this not once again *gaebyeok*?" (Source: *Yongdam Yusa*)
"How could you possibly know Sangjenim of Heaven's Golden Palace?" (Source: *Yongdam Yusa*)
"Call me your father." (Source: *Dowon Giseo*)

Jesus was the Son that the Father sent to this world. The Bible claims that the Spirit of God descended like a dove and a voice from heaven said, "This is my Son whom I love." But that very Father had Eastern Learning established in order to start a totally different and new cosmic history in the eastern land. According to the teachings, a mysterious disease will hit the global village in the future, ruining the Early Heaven's civilizations and opening the door to a new cosmic era and new cosmic order. It will be "once again *gaebyeok*." The teachings proclaimed this idea of *gaebyeok* and the coming advent of Sangjenim, the main character of cosmic politics.

When Choe Je-u met Sangjenim's Holy Spirit, he was told to receive a thirteen-word mantra and educate people with it. The mantra goes: *Si-cheon-ju Jo-hwa-jeong Yeong-se-bul-mang-man-sa-ji*.

By the way, the message of *si-cheon-ju* ("serving the lord of heaven") was later distorted into *in-nae-cheon* ("Within the human, you will find God"). In tandem with the distortion of the message, the name 'Eastern Learning' was also changed to 'Cheondogyo.' All school textbooks, including those for college students, carried this distorted content, hiding from anyone the truth of: the starting point of modern

19세기 후반에는 3백만 동학교도가 있었고, 농민군 60만이 일어났습니다. 동학군이 '개혁을 하라. 5만 년 수운受運, 5만 년 운을 받는다'고 띠를 두르고, 죽창 하나 들고 일어났습니다. 그러나 동학군은 조선과 일본의 군대에게 무참하게 죽음을 당했습니다. 그리하여 고마나루 쪽 금강이 6개월 동안 피로 물들었습니다. 당시 동학군은 공주 우금치에서 고개를 넘어 부여를 향해 진군하려 했는데, 녹두장군에게 그날은 진군을 멈추고 허기진 군사를 쉬게 해야 한다고 했습니다. 그런데 일본군이 매복하고 있다가 미국에서 입수한 최신 기관단총을 쏘아서 시체가 시체 위에 겹치고 겹쳐서 핏빛으로 변했다고 합니다. 그렇게 동학이 무너져 버렸습니다.

그런데 동학은 무엇인가? 동녘 동東 자에 배울 학學, 왜 교가 아니고 도도 아닌가? 동은 해가 뜨는 쪽 밝은 방향을 말합니다.

본래 동이라는 한자는 물건을 묶은 형상을 나타내는데, 이것은 '중심이나, 흔들리지 않는다, 근본이다' 이겁니다. 그래서 동은 본래 이 세계의 중심, 우주의 중심, 사물의 중심을 의미합니다.

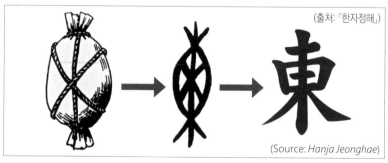

(Source: Hanja Jeonghae)

'동東' 자의 유래: 짐 보따리를 묶은 모양 |
The origin of the character *dong* (東, "east") : the shape of a bound parcel

history; the news from this great city of Gyeongju of a coming new world; the notion of proclaiming a new history.

In the late nineteenth century, Eastern Learning had three million followers, and from these rose a peasant army of six hundred thousand. The Eastern Learning army rose in revolt with bamboo spears and headbands, asserting that if they reformed the country, the destiny of the next fifty thousand years would be theirs. However, they were ruthlessly crushed by the government forces of Joseon and Japan, turning the Geumgang River of Goma Dock blood-red for six months. What happened was that the Eastern Learning army was to cross through the pass from Ugeumchi of Gongju toward Buyeo, but the Eastern Learning army leader Jeon Bong-jun was advised to stop advancing farther that day and let the hungry soldiers rest. Then, the Japanese army ambushed them, firing the latest machineguns acquired from America, choking the area with blood and heaps of dead bodies. That is how Eastern Learning collapsed.

Then what is Eastern Learning (in Korean "Donghak")? Why was it called 'learning' instead of 'teaching' or 'dao'? 'East' indicates the direction of the sun's rising, a bright direction.

Originally, the hanja character *dong* (東 "east") depicted the shape of a bound parcel, which means "a center," "not swayed," or "foundation." Therefore, *dong* signifies the center of the world, the center of the universe, or the center of an object.

참동학의 출현

동학의 30만 농민군이 무너지고서 20세기 초엽에 6백만이 다시 일어났습니다.

이 자리에 계신 이홍범 박사가 동경대와 하버드대에서 수학하고 그 후 몇 십 년 공부해서 쓴 책이 『아시아 이상주의Asian Millenarianism』입니다. 그 책 마지막 장을 보면 '참동학으로서의 증산도'라는 대목이 나옵니다.

오늘 제가 결론에서 말씀드리고 싶은 것은, **동학의 정신과 무너진 동학의 꿈을 이루는, 완성하는 의미의 참동학**입니다. 참동학 구도자 6백만이 정읍을 중심으로 일어났는데, 앞으로 인류가 인간으로 오시는 천주, 천지의 주인 상제님을 모시고 새로운 우주시대, 새로운 우주역사 시대를 연다는 것입니다.

그것이 '다시 개벽'입니다. 참동학에서 완성한 우주관 체계가 바로 '우주 일 년'입니다.

우주에도 봄여름과 가을겨울이 있습니다. 지금까지 우주 일 년, 129,600년에서 선천 5만 년 봄여름 선천 세상을 살았고, 여름 우주의 끝점에서 이제 가을 우주로 다시 개벽의 새 세상으로 들어갑니다.

The Advent of True Eastern Learning

The peasant army of Eastern Learning, which numbered six hundred thousand, collapsed; but in the early twentieth century, six million people rose up again. Dr. Lee Hong-beom, present here, wrote a book titled *Asian Millenarianism* after studying at the University of Tokyo and Harvard University and then conducting research for decades. In the last chapter of the book, there is a section titled "Jeung San Do as the True Eastern Learning."

What I would like to discuss in today's conclusion is True Eastern Learning being a perfector that will reestablish the spirit of Eastern Learning and accomplish Eastern Learning's shattered dream. The six million practioners of True Eastern Learning rose in Jeongeup with the belief that humanity will initiate a new cosmic age or an age of new cosmic history, and serve the Lord of Heaven who would incarnate as a human—that is, Sangjenim, the master of heaven and earth.

That is, "once again *gaebyeok*." The concept of a "cosmic year" is the cosmology completed by True Eastern Learning.

In the universe, there is also spring, summer, autumn, and winter. In the cycle of a cosmic year, which spans 129,600 earth years, humanity has lived, so far, fifty thousand earth years during the Early Heaven's spring and summer seasons. Now, humanity is standing at the end point of cosmic summer, and it is time to enter the cosmic autumn, a new world of "once again *gaebyeok*."

이제 다가오는 후천개벽을 앞두고 우주의 주재자 상제님께서 우주 질서를 잃진 세상에서 바로 세우기 위해서, 선천 상극의 부조화, 불균형, 갈등과 전쟁, 원한의 역사, 선천 상극의 질서를 마감하고 모든 것이 이상적인 균형과 조화를 이루는 우주의 가을철 후천개벽, 그 새 세상 역사 문을 여시기 위해서 인간 세상에 오신다는 것입니다.

선 천		후 천
부조화·불균형 갈등·전쟁 원한의 역사	상제님 강세	이상적인 균형과 조화의 우주 가을철
상극相克		상생相生

그래서 동학의 1차 결론은 '이제 모든 종교 시대는 끝나고 무극대도 닦아내니 5만 년 운수가 열린다'는 것입니다.

Now, with the Later Heaven Gaebyeok ahead, Sangjenim, the Ruler of the Universe, came to this world in order to set right the cosmic order in humanity's world—that is, to put an end to the Early Heaven's order of *sanggeuk* ("mutual conflict") characterized by disharmony, imbalance, conflicts, wars, and a history of resentment, and to open the door of a new world and a new history in cosmic autumn's Later Heaven Gaebyeok wherein everything will be in an ideal balance and harmony.

Early Heaven		Later Heaven
sanggeuk – disharmony, imbalance, conflicts, wars, and a history of resentment	Sangjenim's incarnation	*sangsaeng* – cosmic autumn with an ideal balance and harmony

Thus, the first core conclusion of Eastern Learning is: Now, the era of all religions is to end, so cultivate and purify yourselves with the Supreme Dao of Mugeuk and the destiny of the next fifty thousand years will be yours.

"무극대도 닦아내니 오만년지 운수로다." (『용담유사』)

앞으로 이 지구촌 인류의 보편적인 새로운 생활문화라는 것은 무엇인가? 그것은 종교가 아니라 무극대도입니다.

그런데 이 무극이라는 것은 바로 이 우물 정井 자 문화, 소도문화를 상징하는 우주의 원십자입니다. 그것을 사정방으로 연결하다 보니까 절을 상징하는 만 자가 되는 것입니다. 우물 정 자의 근본, 우주의 원십자 바로 무극대도 세상입니다. 「천부경」으로 말하면 일적십거一積十鉅, 우주의 봄철에 일태극의 기운, 일태극수一太極水가 분열하면서 여름 불의 계절을 거쳐서, 이 가을 우주의 원십자의 진리의 이상이 실제 현실화되는 것입니다.

그것은 지축이 서야 이루어집니다. 우주의 몸체를 상징하는 첨성대가 지금 기울어져 있습니다. 지축이 기울어진 것처럼 23도 5분이 기울어졌어요. 이선 정말로 신묘하다고 봅니다.

첨성대를 만든 장인은 천문을 통달했고, 지난 1만 년의 환국·배달·조선 이후 우주광명의 역사문화, 수학, 기하학 등 여러 가지 인류의 지혜가 이 첨성대에 총합이 되어 있는 것입니다.

"Cultivate and purify yourselves with the Supreme Dao of Mugeuk and the destiny of the next fifty thousand years will be yours." (Source: *Yongdam Yusa*)

What will be the new and universal life culture of humanity in the global village? The answer is not a religion, but the Supreme Dao of Mugeuk. Mugeuk is the primal cross of the universe, symbolizing the culture related to the character *jeong* (井 "water well") and *sodo* culture. When the primal cross (+) is stretched in four directions, it becomes a *man* (卍) character symbolizing a Buddhist temple. The coming world will be the world of the Supreme Dao of Mugeuk, Mugeuk being the foundation of the character *jeong* (井 "water well") and the primal cross of the universe. Just as the phrase from *Cheonbu Gyeong* asserts, "One accumulates and opens as Ten," in the cosmic spring the energy of one-Taegeuk, one-Taegeuk-water divides, and after going through the cosmic summer, the season of the fire element, the ideal world of the primal cross of the universe comes to pass in cosmic autumn.

Such a world will become a reality only after the straightening of the earth's axis. Cheomseongdae Observatory, symbolizing the body of universe, is currently a bit tilted. It is tilted by 23.5 degrees, like the earth's axis. Such a coincidence is indeed mysterious. The master craftsmen who built Cheomseongdae Observatory must have been well-versed in astronomy. Besides, a collection of humanity's wisdom for almost ten thousand years—from the time of Hwanguk, Baedal, and Dangun Joseon, including the history and culture of cosmic radiance, algebra, and geometry—was integrated into Cheomseongdae Observatory.

The inside of Cheomseongdae Observatory is tilted by 23.5 degrees, like the earth's axis.
(Source: Documentary "Separate Notes on Cheomseongdae Observatory")

참동학의 출발점 보천교

그런데 이 동학을 계승한 참동학 보천교 6백만 신도가 왜 정읍에서 일어났는가? 정읍井邑이라는 지명에도 우물 정 자가 들어 있습니다. 보천교에서 정읍에 동아시아에서 가장 큰 궁전 십일전十一殿을 지었습니다. 그런데 교주 차경석車京石(1880~1936) 성도가 세상을 떠나자마자 일제가 강제 해체, 처분해서 뜯어다가 옮겨놓은 것이 지금 서울 종로2가에 있는 대한민국 불교 본부 조계종의 대웅전입니다.

어찌하여 이것이 기록에 한마디도 안 남고, 대한민국 국민이 이토록 모르고 있을까요? 당시 20세기 초엽 독립운동과 항일저항운동을 다룬 조선일보 기사를 보면 약 54%를 보천교가 차지합니다. 태일문화를 들고 나온 이들 6백만 명이, 9천 년 역사문화의 원형정신 태일을 성취하는 태을 우주노래를 부르던 그 사람들이 바로 상해 임시정부 독립자금을 거반 다 대었습니다.

The Starting Point of True Eastern Learning: Bocheongyo

By the way, why did six million practioners of Bocheongyo, regarded as the True Eastern Learning that succeeded Eastern Learning, rise up at Jeongeup? In fact, the place name 'Jeongeup' (井邑) contains the *jeong* character (井). Bocheongyo built, in Jeongeup, Sibiljeon Palace, the biggest palace in East Asia. However, as soon as Cha Gyeong-seok (1880-1936), a disciple of Sangjenim and the leader of Bocheongyo, passed away, the Japanese colonial government forcibly disassembled the palace, and parts of it were later used to construct the main hall, named 'Daeungjeon,' of the Jogye Order, the leading sect of Korean Buddhism, currently located in Jongno 2-ga Seoul.

Then how did it happen that there is not a single record of such a fact and few Koreans know about it?

Of the news articles about Koreans' independence and anti-Japanese movements of the early twentieth century mentioned in a major Korean daily, *Joseon Ilbo*, about fifty-four percent were related to Bocheongyo. The six million practitioners of Bocheongyo who brought out Taeil culture and who chanted the Taeeul cosmic song to accomplish Taeil, the original spirit of the nine thousand years of history, financed most of the independence movement of the Korean Provisional Government in Shanghai, China.

Currently, some public officials in Jeongeup say that Jeongeup was the mecca of the Korean independence movement during Japanese colonial rule. As a matter of fact, shortly after Gim Gu, President of the Korean Provisional Government, came back from China when Korea was liberated from Japan, he stated that Koreans were very much indebted to Jeongeup and Bocheongyo. On June 3 of the following year, Dr. Syngman Rhee visited Jeongeup and made an important announcement that he supported the establishment of an independent government on the southern part of the Korean Peninsula.

To sum up, the sacrifice and martyrdom of ten million Eastern

지금 정읍에서 공무원들 일부에서는 '정읍은 독립운동의 메카'라고 합니다. 김구金九 선생은 귀국하자마자 '우리가 정읍에 보천교에 신세를 많이 졌다'고 했습니다. 이듬해 6월 3일 날 이승만李承晩 박사가 이 정읍에 와서 '남한만의 단독 정부를 조직하자'는 중대 발표를 했습니다.

근대 새 역사의 기운을 만들어 준 구도자들, 동학과 참동학의 천만 명의 희생과 순도 속에서 오늘의 대한민국 역사가 전개될 수 있었던 것입니다.

태일문화의 완성, 태을주

그러면 태을, 혹은 태일은 궁극적으로 뭘 말하는가? 그것은 **인간 존재의 궁극**입니다. 가을 우주가 오는 지금 그 길목에서, 우주의 질서가 바뀌는 이 대개벽의 전야에서 우리는 왜 잃어버린 9천 년 역사의 뿌리인 시원문화, 원형문화의 소중한 한 소식으로 돌아가야 할까요?

우주의 모든 생명의 근원은 대우주 생명의 바다입니다. 삼신이 주관하는 이 우주 조화생명의 바다를 지기至氣라고도 하고, 현대에서는 에너지, 장(필드) 등 여러 가지로 말합니다.

이 대우주의 조화 바다에는, 신이 없는 곳이 없고 신이 하지 못하는 바가 없습니다. 그것이 구체적인 우리들의 삶의 현상으로 나타나는 게 하늘과 땅과 인간입니다. 바로 이 우주 만물을 삼신과 한 몸이 되어서, 삼신과 한 생명이 되어서, 삼신의 우주광명 자체가 되어서 다스릴 수 있는 사람 그것이 '**홍익인간弘益人間**'입니다.

홍익인간이 되기 위해서는, 한마음을 바로 세우고 이 깊은 어둠을 깨고 나와서, 우주광명의 실체인 삼신 조물주, 우주 삼신의 조화권을 쓰시는 우주 정치의 주인 되시는 삼신상제님을 바르게 알아야 합니다. 동학에서 말하는 '시천주 조화정'을 올바르게 깨달아야 합니다.

앞으로 과학문명의 모든 문제를 극복하는, 지구촌 환경 문제라든지, 모

Learning and True Eastern Learning practioners, the seekers of truth who provided the energy for a new modern history, paved the way for modern Korean history to unfold.

The Taeeulju Mantra: The Completion of Taeil Culture

By the way, what is Taeeul or Taeil culture all about? It indicates the pinnacle of human existence. On the path of cosmic autumn's arrival, and on the eve of the great *gaebyeok* when the cosmic order is about to change, why do we have to go back to the precious news of the lost original culture or the primordial culture that was the root of our nine thousand years of history?

The source of all lives in the universe is the sea of cosmic life. This sea of cosmic life, or the cosmic sea of creation-tranformation under the control of Samsin, is named *jigi* ("ultimate *qi*"), and it is also called in modern-day terms 'energy' or 'field.'

In the cosmic sea of creation-tansformation, there is no place without God and there is nothing that God cannot do. This power of God manifests as concrete real-life phenomena, such as heaven, earth, and humanity. A person who can govern all things in this universe by becoming one body with Samsin, by becoming one life with Samsin, and by becoming Samsin's cosmic radiance itself, is a *hongik ingan* ("human being who fosters far-reaching benefits for humanity").

To become a *hongik ingan*, one should set their mind straight, free themselves of deep darkness, and have a correct understanding of Samsin the Creator, who is the essence of cosmic radiance, or Samsin Sangjenim, who is the master of cosmic politics who wields Samsin's power of creation-transformation. One should have a correct understanding of Eastern Learning's principle of *Si-cheon-ju Jo-hwa-jeong* ("By serving the Lord of Heaven (Sangjenim) who would incarnate as a human, we will initiate an age of new cosmic history.").

In the future, when *gaebyeok* arrives, all the issues of modern civilization—including the environmental problems of the global village,

든 종교의 갈등, 또는 부익부 빈익빈 같은 오늘의 자본주의의 어려움을 총체적으로 극복하는 개벽이 옵니다. 그 개벽은, 선천 상극의 우주 질서에서 오는 원한과 갈등, 너무도 억울하게 음해를 받고 일방적으로 공격당해서 죽어간 사람들의 원기寃氣, 원령寃靈이 천지에 꽉 찼기 때문에 그 원한을 풀어주는 해원解寃의 도를 바탕에 깔고 있습니다. 선천 우주자연의 질서인 상극, 불균형, 부조화의 상극을 가을 우주의 성숙을 이루는 생명의 질서, 상생으로 바꿔 줄 때 개벽의 모든 것을 단숨에 이룰 수가 있습니다.

그래서 삼신상제 천주님이 오셔서 당신의 무궁한 무극대도의 조화법을 쓰십니다. 그리하여 진정한 문명개벽, 자연개벽, 궁극의 인간개벽이 이루어지는 것입니다.

태을천太乙天과 치성광여래

태을주는 '5만 년 운수'를 딘 사람이 읽는다는 주문입니다. 태을은 부엇인가?

천상에는 태을천太乙天이 있습니다. 바로 우주 통치자 하나님 원 우리말로 삼신상제님, 유교와 도교에서도 쓰는 상제님이 북두칠성에 계십니다. 그 북두칠성의 머리 두 개의 별에서 직선으로 쭉 뻗으면 거기에 무슨 별이 있어요? 진정으로 움직이지 않는 북녘의 별, 북극성이 있습니다.

그 북극성이 바로 태일 자리이고, 태일신이면서 바로 태을천이라는 우주의 신도세계가 있는 곳입니다. 이것을 불교에서도 아마 천 년에 몇 명이 도통을 했는지 이따금 아는 사람이 있습니다.

religious conflicts, and drawbacks of capitalism such as the widening gap between the rich and the poor—will be universally overcome. Due to the Early Heaven's cosmic order of *sanggeuk*, heaven and earth are filled with bitterness and grief, with conflicts, and with the resentful energy of the grudge-bearing spirits of people who lost lives due to false accusations. The coming *gaebyeok*, therefore, is based on the dao of resolving the bitterness and grief of the Early Heaven. When the Early Heaven's cosmic order of *sanggeuk*, characterized by imbalance and disharmony, is changed into *sangsaeng*, the order of life that will bring maturation in the cosmic autumn, every aspect of *gaebyeok* will be completely fulfilled. Such being the case, Samsin Sangjenim, the Lord of Heaven, will come and wield his power of creation-transformation—that is, his boundless Supreme Dao of Mugeuk.

Then, the *gaebyeok* of civilization and of nature in the true sense, and eventually the *gaebyeok* of humanity, will be attained.

Taeeulcheon and Tejaprabha ("Buddha of Radiant Light")

The Taeeulju Mantra is the mantra chanted by those who are to be blessed with the destiny of the next fifty thousand years. What does 'Taeeul' indicate?

In heaven, there is Taeeulcheon. And God, the Ruler of the Universe, resides in the Big Dipper; God was also called "Samsin Sangjenim" in ancient Korea and "Sangje" in Confucianism and Daoism. Draw a straight line from the two front stars of the Big Dipper and what star do we see? There shines the star of the north, which seems to rarely move, and that is the North Star. The North Star is the place of Taeil, where the spirit realm of the universe, i.e. Taeeulcheon, is located, and the Taeil Spirit is in Taeeulcheon. It seems some Buddhist monks in Silla attained enlightenment during the nearly millenium-long era of Silla because they knew these facts.

"북극성은 태일신이 있는 태을천太乙天"

The North Star is where Taeeulcheon is located, the place where the Taeil Spirit resides.

여름 / summer
spring 봄
North Star Taeil
북극성 太一
가을 / autumn
winter
겨울

청도 운문사雲門寺에 가보면 칠성신들을 그려놨는데 거기에 치성광여래熾盛光如來가 있습니다. 그런데 불가에서도 이것을 제대로 아는 사람이 없습니다. 몇 십 년 도 닦아서 사는 사람도, 한평생 도 닦은 도승 흉내 내는 사람도 물어보면 치성광여래의 실체를 모릅니다.

이 치성광여래가 대우주의 **생명의 핵**, 대우주 광명 조화 그 신성의 핵을 뭐라고 했는가? 음양의 언어로 **율려**律呂라 했습니다.

만물을 움직이게 하는, 우리들로 하여금 춤을 추게 하는 양의 생명, 율동, 그것을 율律이라 합니다. 율동律動이라고 할 때 이 율을 씁니다. 그리고 우리의 마음을 대자연의 마음처럼 고요하게, 본래의 우주 생명 의식으로, 영원불멸의 생명의 마음으로, 평화의 마음으로, 우리 모두가 한마음이 되도록, 하나의 일체의식을 갖도록 해 주는 진정한 불멸의 생명의식, 일체의식, 그리고 그 한마음. 깨달음, 도통의 마음. 그것을 여呂라 합니다. 그래서 율동여정律動呂靜이라는 말을 합니다.

하루 시간의 경계에서 보면 율려가 얼마 작용하고, 1년이면 얼마 작용한다는 율려 도수가 있습니다. 이 내용이 『정역正易』에도 나옵니다. 다만 이 율려는 우주정신, 우주 생명의 핵이기 때문에 태을주를 오래 읽으면, 한마

치성광여래 熾盛光如來 | 청도 운문사. 칠성신앙을 불교에서 수용하여 북극성을 여래如來로 인격화한 것
Tejaprabha ("Buddha of Radiant Light")
Unmunsa Temple, Cheongdo County
Tejaprabha ("Buddha of Radiant Light") is a personification of the North Star after Buddhism accommodated the popular faith in Seven Stars.

In Unmunsa Temple of Cheongdo County, Tejaprabha ("Buddha of Radiant Light") has been drawn along with the spirits of the Seven Stars. However, few in Buddhism know Tejaprabha well. Neither people who have cultivated dao for decades nor those Buddhist monks who, after cultivating themselves throughout their lives, have attained spiritual enlightenment know the true nature of Tejaprabha ("Buddha of Radiant Light") when asked.

What did Tejaprabha ("Buddha of Radiant Light") call the core of life in the universe, or the divine essence of the cosmic radiance's creation-transformation? It was named 'Yullyeo' in the language of yin and yang.

The life force or the rhythm of yang that makes everything moves, and us dance, is called '*yul.*' This character *yul* is used in *yulddong*, which means "rhythm" in Korean. And *lyeo* (sometimes used as *yeo*) is a truly undying life awareness, a sense of oneness, one mind, awakening, or enlightened mind, that enables us: to be calm in the way of nature's mindset; to have a sense of the original cosmic life; to possess the mindset of life without death, a peaceful mind; and to become of one mind and feel like a unified one. That is why we use the expression *yulddong yeojeong* ("moving *yul*, still *yeo*") in Korean.

Speaking of *yullyeo*, there is the Yullyeo Dosu, which shows how

음으로 잘 읽으면 만병이 범치 못합니다.

신라가 무너지는 과정과 시두

신라가 무너지는 과정을 보면, 나중에 내물왕계奈勿王系하고 김춘추 김씨 계열 사이에 왕권 다툼이 생겨서 150년 동안 왕이 한 스무 명씩 바뀝니다. 그러면서 신라가 망합니다.

그런데 37대 선덕왕宣德王이 시두時痘에 걸려서 발진이 생기면서 13일 만에 세상을 떠납니다. 그리고 문성왕文聖王(신라 46대 왕)이 또 7일 만에 시두로 돌아가십니다.

왕조의 역사가 문 닫고 새로운 역사가 올 때, 인류 문명의 거대한 전환기, 그 역사 경계에서는 무엇이 왔는가? 고대에서 중세, 중세에서 근세, 근세에서 현대로 넘어오는 과정에서도 반드시 이 시두가 옵니다. 그래서 '앞으로 시두가 없다가 대폭발이 되면 내 세상이 오는 줄 알아라'는 상제님 말씀이 있습니다. 시두가 대발하면 삼신 상제님의 개벽 세상으로 급진합니다. 이 것이 참동학 증산도의 『도전』에 나와 있는 내용입니다.

many times *yullyeo* functions within one day and one year. This is described in *Jeongyeok*. *Yullyeo* is the core of the cosmic mind and cosmic life, so if a person chants the Taeeulju Mantra devotedly for a long time with one mind, no disease can attack them.

The Process of the Silla Dynasty's Collapse, and Smallpox

Concerning the process of the Silla Dynasty's collapse, a fierce struggle was launched between the descendants of King Naemul and King Muyeol (Gim Chunchu) for the throne in the dynasty's late era, with twenty kings being crowned over a period of 150 years, thus accelerating the country's decline.

By the way, the thirty-seventh ruler of Silla, King Seondeok, contracted smallpox, rashes erupting, and passed away in thirteen days. In a later era, King Munseong (forty-sixth king of Silla) was also infected with smallpox, passing away in seven days. Then what customarily happened at pivotal points in history, such as great turning points of human civilization or the times when one dynasty came to an end and another started? At every transition from ancient to medieval, from medieval to early modern, and from early modern to modern times, there would be an outbreak of smallpox without fail. Concerning this, Sangjenim said, "When smallpox erupts in the days to come, know that my world has arrived." In fact, when smallpox breaks out on a large scale, the world will rapidly transition to Samsin Sangjenim's world of *gaebyeok*. That is what is said in the Dojeon ("Holy Scriptures of Dao") of True Eastern Learning, Jeung San Do.

태을주의 '훔치'와 그 완성

太乙呪

吽哆
훔 치 　　太乙天 上元君 吽哩哆哪都來 吽哩喊哩娑婆訶
吽哆　　　태을천 상원군 훔리치야도래 훔리함리사파하
훔 치

태을주를 한번 잘 읽어보세요. '훔치 훔치 태을천 상원군 훔리치야도래 훔리함리사파하.'

이 '훔吽'이라는 것은 이 대우주 **생명의 핵**입니다. 우주의 모든 소리의 근원입니다. 여기에 대해서 도통한 분이 일본에서 가장 큰 절, 엔랴쿠지, 뻗칠 연延 자에다가 책력이라는 력曆 자, 연력사延曆寺에 있었습니다. 그분이 쿠카이(空海) 스님입니다.

이 쿠카이 스님이 대우주의 생명의 근원소리 훔을 밝혔습니다. 그래서 『훔자의吽字義』를 비롯, 여러 책이 나왔고, 영어로도 번역이 되었습니다. 이 법신法身과 화신化身과 보신報身, 우주의 모든 부처님, 팔만대장경, 깨달음, 진리, 그 생명의 핵이 한 글자로 훔입니다.

쿠카이空海 | 774~835. 일본 헤이안 시대 승려
저서: 『훔자의吽字義』
Kukai (774-835):
A Buddhist monk of the Heian period in
Japan, he authored *The Meaning of Hoom*
(『吽字義』).

The 'Hoomchi' in the Taeeulju Mantra and Its Completion

The Taeeulju Mantra

吽哆

太乙天 上元君 吽哩哆唧都來 吽哩喊哩娑婆訶

吽哆

Hoom-chi
    Tae-eul-cheon Sang-won-gun
    Hoom-ri-chi-ya-do-rae Hoom-ri-ham-ri-sa-pa-ha
Hoom-chi

Read the Taeeulju Mantra once carefully: "*Hoom-chi Hoom-chi Tae-eul-cheon Sang-won-gun Hoom-ri-chi-ya-do-rae Hoom-ri-ham-ri-sa-pa-ha*"

'*Hoom* 吽' is the core of cosmic life. It is the source of all sounds in the universe. The person who attained enlightenment about the significance of the *hoom* sound was a monk in the biggest temple in Japan: Enryaku-ji (*en* (延) means "extend"; *ryaku* (曆), "calendar"; *ji* (寺), "temple"). The name of this monk was 'Kukai.'

Monk Kukai expounded upon *hoom*, the source sound of cosmic life. Related books, including *The Meaning of Hoom*, have been published, and some of them have been translated into English. The Dharma Body of, the Transformation Body of, and the Body of the Bliss of Buddha; all buddhas of the universe; the Tripitaka Koreana; enlightenment; the truth; and the core of life—all of these are contained in a single character: *hoom*.

『훔자의吽字義』| 우주 생명의 근원소리 '훔吽'을 밝힌 책
The Meaning of Hoom (吽字義) is a book that expounds upon the source sound of cosmic life: *hoom* (吽).

대우주 생명의 핵, 모든 소리를 낳는 근원소리 훔吽

그리고 '치哆'라는 것은 이 우주의 생명의 근원, 성령의 근원 그것과 내 몸이 하나가 된다, 일체가 된다, 신과 일체가 된다, 한 몸이 된다는 것입니다. 훔치 훔치 태을천 상원군 훔리치야도래 훔리함리사파하.

칠성과 삼신문화의 원점, 그 궁극의 역사문화의 지향인 태일은 북극성에 계시는 태을천 상원군님이십니다. 전라도 함평咸平에 계시던 김경소라는 분은 50년 동안 주문 읽고, 기도를 했습니다. 그래서 '태을천 상원군을 덧붙여 읽어라'는 계시를 받았습니다. '훔리치야도래 훔리함리사파하' 위에 붙인 '태을천 상원군'이라는 여섯 자가 천상에서 내려온 것입니다. 그 뒤에 상제님께서 훔 자, 치 자를 덧붙여서 태을주를 완성해 주셨습니다.

한민족 통일과 인류 문화 대통일을 향해

앞으로 실제 남북통일은 어떻게 될까요? 통일의 그 위대한 비전은 무엇일까요? 동양 신교 우주론은 「천부경」과 주역인데, 결론은 무엇인가요?

'종어간終於艮 시어간始於艮'입니다. 동북 간방艮方에서 마무리가 되고, 이 간방에서 새롭게 시작이 됩니다. 이 선천 상극의 갈등, 최후의 역사전쟁이 앞으로 38선에서 실제 상황으로 전개됩니다.

우리가 실크로드 문화를 보면 이 지구촌 동서남북을 소통시킨 북방 유목민, 바로 그 위대한 한 혈통이 신라에 와서 이곳 왕도에서 김씨 왕조, 서른여덟 명의 왕이 나왔습니다. 이들이 삼국통일을 했지만 그것은 **미완의 통일**입니다. 북쪽과 남쪽 두 개 나라로 다시 대치한 남북국 시대였기 때문입니다.

Hoom (吽): The core of cosmic life and the source sound that
gives birth to all other sounds.

Chi (哆) signifies that the source of cosmic life—or the source of the
Holy Spirit—and one's own body become one, becoming one with God.
 *Hoom-chi Hoom-chi Tae-eul-cheon Sang-won-gun Hoom-ri-chi-
ya-do-rae Hoom-ri-ham-ri-sa-pa-ha*
 Taeil—the starting point of the cultures of the Seven Stars and Samsin and also the ultimate destination of those cultures—is Taeeulcheon
Sangwongun of the North Star. Concerning Taeeulcheon Sangwongun,
a man named 'Gim Gyeong-so' in Hampyeong County, Jeolla-do Province, chanted a mantra and prayed for fifty years. In the end, he received
a revelation that he should attach *Tae-eul-cheon Sang-won-gun* to the
mantra. Therefore, the six syllables of *Tae-eul-cheon Sang-won-gun*,
added before *Hoom-ri-chi-ya-do-rae Hoom-ri-ham-ri-sa-pa-ha*, descended from heaven. Later, Sangjenim completed the Taeeulju Mantra
by adding two characters: *hoom* and *chi*.

The Unifications of the Korean People and of Humanity's Cultures
 In the future, how will the unification of South and North Korea actually be accomplished? What is the best prospect for the two Koreas'
unification? The cosmology of the East's Spirit Teaching is based on
Cheonbu Gyeong and the *Book of Changes* (*I Ching*/*Yi Jing*), and what
is their conclusive message? It is that everything ends in the direction
of Gan (艮, "Northeast") and starts anew in the direction of Gan. In
line with this message, the climax of the Early Heaven's conflicts derived from its cosmic order of *sanggeuk*—that is, the last war over history—will actually unfold in the region of the thirty-eighth parallel.
 If I may describe the Silla Dynasty in terms of the Silk Road culture:
one of the great bloodlines of the northern nomads who faciliated exchanges between peoples in the global village moved to Silla, where they
produced thirty-eight kings from the Gim Clan in Silla's capital. They

인간으로 오신 강증산 상제님이 '장차 한국이 제일 좋다'(道典 5:388)고 하신 것처럼 앞으로 세계일가 통일이 이루어집니다. "만국활계남조선萬國活計南朝鮮이요 청풍명월금산사淸風明月金山寺라 문명개화삼천국文明開化三千國이요 도술운통구만리道術運通九萬里라."(道典 5:306:6) 앞으로 문명은 3천 국으로 열리니까 나라가 훨씬 더 많아집니다.

중국도 이번에 개벽을 하면서 원시반본, 뿌리를 찾아서 쪼개집니다. 미국도 쪼개지고 모든 나라가 그 뿌리와 근본을 찾아서 쪼개집니다.

앞으로 인류의 새로운 문명, 역사시대를 열어줄 활방活方이 있는 곳은 지구촌에서 남쪽 조선밖에 없습니다.

맑은 바람, 밝은 달, 이 청풍명월淸風明月이라는 것은 충청도인데, 원래 상제님 도의 본부가 태전에 있습니다. 태전은 지리적으로 역국逆局이 가장 큰 곳이라고 합니다. 청풍명월의 금산사金山寺, 이 신라에서 미륵불을 섬겨왔던 화랑의 정신, 진정한 불교문화, 미래적인 불교의 그 위대한 정신을 표상하는 곳이 바로 금산사입니다.

Geumsansa Temple is where authentic Buddhist culture and the spirit of future Buddhism are alive.

진정한 불교문화, 미래 불교의 정신이 살아있는 금산사

managed to unify the three ancient kingdoms of Korea, but it was an incomplete unification because another era of confrontation started between North State and South State, at the same time as the unification.

As Gahng Jeung-san Sangjenim, who incarnated as a human, declared, in the future, Korea will become the most auspicious of all lands and the world will be unified as one family. Sangjenim also stated, "The means of saving the world lies in South Joseon. The land of fresh breeze and bright moon fulfills the dream of Geumsansa Temple. The new civilization of autumn blooms into three thousand nations. The grand destiny of the dao mastery civilization ripples to the ends of the universe" (Dojeon 5:166:5). Just as he stated that the new civilization would bloom into three thousand nations, we will have far more countries in the future. At the time of this coming *gaebyeok*, China will split apart as part of a search for their roots, following the principle of seeking out the beginning and returning to the origin. The US will be no exception, and all other countries will split apart as part of a search for their roots and origins.

South Joseon will be the only place in the global village that has the means to initiate a new civilization and a new era of history for humanity in the coming days. The land of fresh breeze and bright moon, mentioned before, indicates Chungcheong-do Province. In fact, the headquarters of Sangjenim's dao is located in Taejeon, Chungcheong-do Province. It is said that Taejeon is the place that demonstrates a larger reversal of water flows from its original course than any other place, according to the principle of the earth. And Geumsansa Temple is the very place that represents the Hwarang Knights' spirit of worshipping Maitreya Buddha, authentic Buddhist culture, and the great spirit of future Buddhism.

만 국 활 계 남 조 선　　청 풍 명 월 금 산 사
萬國活計南朝鮮이요 淸風明月金山寺라

지구촌 모든 나라를 살려내는 법방은 남쪽 조선에 있고
맑은 바람 밝은 달의 금산사로다. (道典 5:306)

금산사는 통일신라시대 진표眞表(734~?) 스님이 '나를 이 모양 이 형상대로 받아 세워라'는 미륵님, 도솔천 천주님 명을 받아서 세웠습니다. 미륵님이 한 발은 김제군 금산사 자리를 딛고, 한 발은 변산邊山을 딛고 천지 사람처럼 법신으로 서셨다는 것입니다. 그래서 그걸 축약해서 세계에서 가장 큰 실내불 미륵부처님을 세운 곳이 금산사입니다. 거기는 미륵님이 여의주를 쥐고 계십니다.

　천지 뜻을 뜻대로 이루시는 분이 바로 불교에서 말하는 도솔천 천주님이고, 그 천주님이 내내 상제님입니다. 이것을 당나라 때 신선 여동빈呂洞賓(798~?)이 깨친 깃입니다. 여동빈이 바로 '상제님이 미륵이다, 그 미륵이 바로 상제님이다' 하는 것을 깨달았던 것입니다. 원래 우주의 도의 주인은 그 한 분일 것 아닙니까?

진표眞表율사 | 734 ~ ?. 미륵님(도솔천 천주님)의 천명을 받아 금산사에 미륵불상을 조성함.
Precept Master Jinpyo (734 - ?)
After receiving a heavenly mandate from Maitreya Buddha (Lord of Tushita Heaven), Jinpyo built the statue of Maitreya Buddha at Geumsansa Temple.

"The means of saving the world lies in South Joseon. The land of fresh breeze and bright moon fulfills the dream of Geumsansa Temple." (Dojeon 5:166:5)

Jinpyo (734-?), a Buddhist monk of the Unified Silla era, constructed Geumsansa Temple after receiving a mandate from Maitreya Buddha, the Lord of Tushita Heaven, to build a statue exactly like the appearance of Maitreya that Jinpyo beheld when his heavenly eye opened. That is, the Maitreya Buddha stood with one foot on Geumsansa Temple at Gimje-gun County, and the other on Mt. Byeonsan, manifesting himself in his dharma body. The size of the Maitreya statue erected in Geumsansa Temple, though scaled down, was the biggest indoor Maitreya Buddha statue in the world. The Maitreya Buddha in that temple is holding a cin-tamani, a wish-fulfilling jewel. The one who effortlessly accomplishes the wishes of heaven and earth is the Lord of Tushita Heaven mentioned in Buddhism, and this Lord of Tushita Heaven is also Sangjenim.

That is what Lu Dongbin (798-?), an immortal of the Tang Dynasty, perceived. He realized that Sangjenim is Maitreya Buddha; Maitreya Buddha is the very Sangjenim. The original master of the cosmic dao is supposed to be only him, is he not?

여동빈呂洞賓 | 798 ~ ?. 당나라 신선. 상제님과 미륵 불이 한 분임을 밝힘.
Lu Dongbin (798 -?).
An immortal of the Tang Dynasty, he revealed that Sangjenim and Maitreya Buddha are the same being.

전 세계, 온 우주가 이번에 일가 한집안 문화권으로 새로 태어납니다. 총체적으로 인류 문명이 대혁신 되는 통일의 비전을 앞두고 시두 대발의 시간이 성큼성큼 다가오고 있습니다. 미국에서는 행정부와 국방부에서 이것을 염려해서 주한 미군이 수년 전에 시두 백신을 다 맞았어요.

시두를 계기로 해서 인간은 어둠에서, 크고 작은 그런 죄업에서 나와 이 우주 생명, 광명 그 자체로 살아야 됩니다. 이것이 9천 년 소도 제천문화의 근본정신입니다. 그리고 항상 끊임없이 새로운 생명이 솟구치는 이 소도 생명의 나무를 세우는 의식을 가져야 합니다. 이때는 원시로 반본하는 때라, 우리가 이 근본, 원형 역사문화 정신을 복구할 때 신교문화, 9천 년 역사문화가 부활하면서 새 시대를 여는 하나의 기초 토대를 놓게 된다는 것을 저는 확신합니다.

The entire world, or the whole universe, will be born again as one family under a single culture at the time of this coming *gaebyeok*. In light of the vision of the coming unification when humanity's civilization will be comprehensively reformed, it is clear that the time is fast approaching when smallpox will break out on a large scale. Greatly concerned, the US government had all members of the US forces stationed in Korea get vaccinated against smallpox years ago.

With smallpox as an impetus, humans should live as cosmic life—as cosmic radiance itself—breaking out of darkness and freeing ourselves of great and small sinful acts. This is the fundamental spirit of the culture that offered heavenly rituals at *sodo*s for nine thousand years. And humanity should also have the consciousness to erect the *sodo*'s tree of life where new life force is continuously welling up. Now is the era of seeking out the beginning and returning to the origin. I am sure that when we revive the origin and the spirit of the primordial history and culture, the Spirit Teaching culture and the nine-thousand-year history will revive, creating a foundation upon which to initiate a new era.

결론

이 모든 것을 이루는 것은 태일문화, 소도 제천문화에서는 바로 '큰마음' 입니다. 천지부모와 한마음, 한 몸, 한 생명이 되는 큰마음입니다. 그런 큰마음을 갖고 천지조화의 신성을 자기 스스로 체험하고, 아픈 몸을 건강하게, 삐뚤어진 정신을 건강한 마음으로 바꾸어야 합니다. 그 다음에 가정 질서를 반듯하게 복원하고, 말할 수 없이 국론이 갈라져 있는 우리 사회를 통합해 나가야 할 것입니다.

우리는 새로운 역사를 열기 위해서 일관되게 한눈팔지 않고 진정한 마음으로, 일심으로 오직 앞을 보면서 밀고 나가야 한다고 봅니다. 오늘 일관되게 주장하는 이 대우주의 역사, 문화, 우리들의 삶의 목적, 깨달음, 기도, 행복, 그것은 한 글자도 맑을 환桓, 우주광명 환입니다.

삼신상제, 조물주 하나님의 신과 생명 그 영체, 성령체와 한 몸이 된 우주광명인간으로, 이 우주의 가장 지극한 존재로 거듭나서 가을 우주의 노래 태을주와, 가을 우주의 새 역사 개벽의 노래 '시천주 조화정 영세불망만사지'를 생활 속에서 늘 함께하시기 바랍니다.

오늘 신라 천년 왕도 경주에서 6촌장의 고향 솟터 문화의 큰 뜻, 우주 광명의 역사의식, 신관, 역사관의 신성한 우주 솟대를 한번 힘차게 세우면서, 앞으로 통일문화 시대의 주역이 되실 것을 축원합니다.

감사합니다.

Conclusion

What makes all of this possible in Taeil culture and *sodo* culture is "great mind." It is a mind that becomes one mind, one body, and one life with heaven and earth, our parents. With such a great mind, one should experience on one's own the divinity of heaven and earth's creation-transformation, and change their sick body into a healthy one and their twisted mind into sound one. After that, the order within one's family should be restored to uprightness, and our society of severely split public opinions should start to become united.

To initiate a new history, we have only to keep consistently going forward with an authentic mind—with one mind—without becoming distracted. The key word of today's lecture—which has covered a variety of areas including cosmic history, culture, the purpose of our life, awakening, prayer, and happiness—is the word *hwan* ("brightness," "cosmic radiance").

I wish foremost that all of you will be reborn as the people of cosmic radiance who become one with the divinity, life, and holy body of Samsin Sangjenim, or of the Creator God, as the most sublime beings of the universe; and that you will live always with the Taeeulju Mantra, which is the song of cosmic autumn, and with "*Si-cheon-ju Jo-hwa-jeong Young-se-bul-mang Man-sa-ji*," which is the song of *gaebyeok*, to initiate a new history at the time of cosmic autumn.

Today, in Gyeongju, the capital of Silla for a thousand years, we have raised up, with all our strength, cosmic sacred pillars supporting: the significance of elevated site-related culture in the home of the six village heads; the historical consciousness of cosmic radiance; the viewpoints of spirits and history. I wish for you all to become leading protagonists in the coming era of a culture of unification.

Thank you.

동방 한국사의 올바른 국통맥

삼성조 시대
9222년 전

환국 (BCE 7197~BCE 3897)
7대 환인 : 3301년간(조화시대)

5922년 전

배달 (BCE 3897~BCE 2333)
18대 환웅 : 1565년간(교화시대)

4358년 전

조선 (BCE 2333~BCE 238)
47대 단군 : 2096년간(치화시대)

열국 시대
2264년 전

북부여 (BCE 239~BCE 58)

동부여 (BCE 86~CE 494)
남삼한 (BCE 194~CE 8)
최씨낙랑국 (BCE 195~CE 37)
동옥저 (BCE 56~?)
동예 (?~CE 245)

사국 시대
2083년 전

고구려 (BCE 58~CE 668)

BCE
CE

백제 (BCE 18~CE 660)
신라 (BCE 57~CE 668)
가야 (CE 42~532)

남북국 시대
1357년 전

대진(발해) (668~926)
후신라(통일신라) (668~935)

1107년 전

고려 (918~1392)

633년 전

조선 (1392~1910)

106년 전

임시정부 (1919~1945)

남북분단 시대
2025년 기준

대한민국 (1948~)
조선민주주의인민공화국(1948~)

지구촌 통일문화 시대
후천 가을개벽 후 천지 광명 문화 시대

Chronology of Korean States and Dynasties

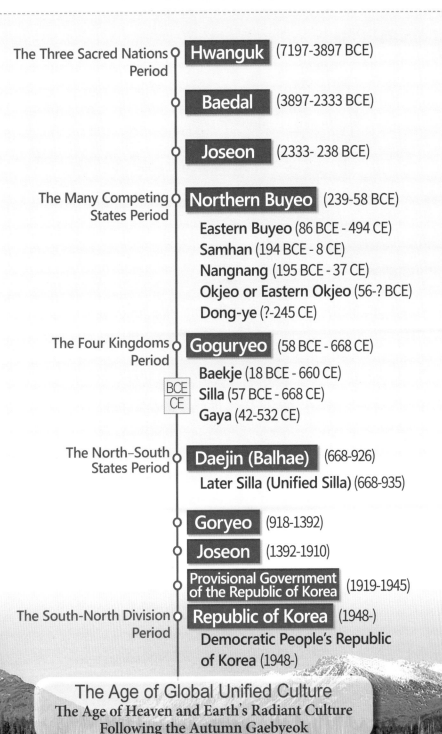

The Three Sacred Nations Period

Hwanguk (7197-3897 BCE)

Baedal (3897-2333 BCE)

Joseon (2333- 238 BCE)

The Many Competing States Period

Northern Buyeo (239-58 BCE)

Eastern Buyeo (86 BCE - 494 CE)
Samhan (194 BCE - 8 CE)
Nangnang (195 BCE - 37 CE)
Okjeo or Eastern Okjeo (56-? BCE)
Dong-ye (?-245 CE)

The Four Kingdoms Period

Goguryeo (58 BCE - 668 CE)

Baekje (18 BCE - 660 CE)

BCE
CE

Silla (57 BCE - 668 CE)
Gaya (42-532 CE)

The North–South States Period

Daejin (Balhae) (668-926)

Later Silla (Unified Silla) (668-935)

Goryeo (918-1392)

Joseon (1392-1910)

Provisional Government of the Republic of Korea (1919-1945)

The South-North Division Period

Republic of Korea (1948-)

Democratic People's Republic of Korea (1948-)

The Age of Global Unified Culture
The Age of Heaven and Earth's Radiant Culture
Following the Autumn Gaebyeok

누구나 쉽게 읽고 함께 감동한다
다양한 판형의『환단고기』10종 출간

인류의 시원사와 한민족 9천년사의
국통맥國統脈을 바로잡는
신교 문화의 정통 도가道家 역사서의 결정판!

1. 역주본『환단고기』: 원본 80,000원 | 축소판 58,000원

2. 현토본『환단고기』: 원본 30,000원 | 축소판 18,000원

3. 보급판『환단고기』: 23,000원

4.『쉽게 읽는 청소년 환단고기』: 원본 25,000원 | 축소판 20,000원

5.『온 가족이 함께 읽는 어린이 환단고기』: 원본 28,000원 | 축소판 18,000원

6. 포켓용『환단고기』: 15,000원